Advance Praise for
SUPERNATURAL CREATIVITY
By Jill Elizabeth Wyckoff

"Every page of this book stretches the reader and pushes them towards action. With great vulnerability and impact Jill is able to communicate the heart of creative freedom. She invites us all to join in this wonderful adventure as she glides between powerful insight, moving stories, active prompts, painting, and poetry. Supernatural Creativity is totally in the groove!"

—**Bradley "Groove" Rapier,** award-winning choreographer / Founder, GROOVE Mindset, https://www.bradleyrapier.com/ @bradleyrapier @groovemindset

"This book had me in a state of childlike awe and wonder from the first chapter! Jill brings a beautiful combination of wisdom from her own deep relationship with the Lord and a playful, simple, childlike view of His creativity! The beauty of God's creativity is how relational it is – it is FOR US! When we step into the creativity that Jill emphatically declares is for all of us to express…people's lives around us will be forever transformed! Let this book stir a hunger in you to tap into that foundational part of your identity – you are a creator, and let God release that through your life and your unique set of circumstances!"

—**Luke Roque**, Roque Productions, https://www.roque-productions.com/

"The space between imagination and manifestation is fraught with giants lurking to distract us from fully manifesting the creativity for which we were designed. Jill's book unleashes you to terrorize every giant that has dared to stand in the way of your creative calling! These pages will inspire you to fully explore your authority in Christ and awaken your creativity in such a way that the world will be in awe of The Creator."

—**Craig Muster,** author of Plunder Darkness,
Executive Coach, International Speaker
https://www.craigmuster.com/ https://www.craigandkarlet.com/

"If you've ever felt the urge to create but didn't quite know how to begin, this book is for you. Using wisdom, wit, and authenticity, Jill breaks down the barriers that often keep us from going after all God has called us to be. An inspiring read for those who love to both ponder and be stirred to action!"

—**Rebecca Friedlander,** filmmaker, songwriter, and author of Finding Beautiful: Discovering Authentic Beauty Around the World.
https://www.rebeccafriedlander.com/

"This is a book for Christians who trust a supernatural God to be at work in their lives but wonder exactly how God's power and grace can make a difference in their creative process. Jill Wyckoff's energy is infectious, and her recommendations are clear and very practical. Looking for courage? For direction? For an invitation to take yourself lightly and God's kingdom seriously? You will appreciate Jill's writing and her speaking, her joy, and her deep, deep faith."

—**Diana Glyer,** artist, speaker, and author of Bandersnatch and Clay in the Potter's Hands. https://www.dianaglyer.com/

"I could not put this book down!! From the very introduction of Jill Wyckoff's book, Supernatural Creativity, I found myself encountering the Holy Spirit with goosebumps and tears. Jill has an ability to articulate profound truths in such a way that the reader is fully engaged and her testimonies will leave you awestruck with our amazing God! Supernatural Creativity is a doorway into a whole new way of seeing yourself as creative, as well as an invitation to let go of all fear that's holding you back from fully expressing God's divine nature. As Jill says in her book, "Fear causes us to take short breaths and live small lives." and I am convinced it's time for us to take deep breaths and live large. Jill's book and her journey will help us do just that!"

—**Heather Nunn**,
USA Director, Sounds of the Nations

"Supernatural Creativity is not a theoretical work or a shallow philosophical discourse. The words have been ground out with an authentic and child-like pursuit of the limitless supply of the abundance of heaven. Jill has lived the message and this book will become impartation for you to function and live from your original intent to administrate the mysteries of the Kingdom of God."

—**Brian Orme**, Founder and President, Kingdomstrate,
https://iborme.com/

"Jill's words ignite in me a more purposeful understanding of the hidden gems of our creative partnership with God. After having some experience walking this out over the years, her book is not just a timely reminder, but a flint that stokes another level of fire to what I am called to put my hands to and how much God, Himself, wants to prosper them. When you see clearly how God chooses to give these treasures to us, not just for us to share in His glory, but more importantly, to watch in awe as the greatest Craftsman, Himself, makes His intended impact with them, you'll never dismiss an assignment again. Be prepared to be inspired, to live a life of releasing all your arrows, with Supernatural Creativity."

—**Lady Dang**, Recording Artist/Songwriter/Multipreneur, Founder, Stay Royal Records, https://linktr.ee/ladydangworld

"Supernatural Creativity is a game-changer. Some books set the stage and others elevate to another level. This book does both. Jill weaves together her thoughts and experiences beautifully. It's like watching an award-winning play on Broadway come to life. Prepare to be elevated in your thoughts about creativity, no matter your level, whether beginner or veteran. This is a *now* book. God is raising up His creative army as I've never seen before and this masterpiece will be required reading for all who answer His call. Well done!"

—**Brae Wyckoff**, Award-winning author, President of Kingdom Creativity International, Director of Kingdom Writers Association, https://www.kingdomcreativityinternational.com

Supernatural

CREATIVITY

Creating with God for Restorative Impact

By

Jill Elizabeth Wyckoff

Editor: Tiffany Vakilian

tiffany@tiffanyvakilian.com

Cover art by Jill Wyckoff

Cover composition by Sharon Marta, Marta Studios

https://www.martastudios.com

Dedication

This book is dedicated to my family, and to everyone who has ever thought they weren't creative. May your soul awaken to the wonder of your design. You are the spitting image of your Daddy-God, the Master Creator of this incredibly complex and beautiful universe. He is wooing you to release the unique creative expression of His heart that He placed in your heart. All of creation is groaning to see it.

Introduction

 L AST WEEK, I did a Zoom training for twenty-five 10th-grade girls on how to finger paint. As a finger painting artist, I have taught this method numerous times to both Christian and secular audiences. I find that no matter who I'm teaching, creativity (in this case, finger painting) opens the door to a broader experience—a Holy one. This particular event was secular, so in preparation, I prayed. "Lord, help me create an atmosphere that will usher in Your presence for those who don't yet know You.

Two days prior to the teaching, I woke with a plan. I knew it was from Him because it wasn't my typical first-morning go-to thought—coffee! Grateful for His faithfulness, I put His plan into action. Now to preface, we are currently in the midst of the Covid-19 Pandemic, extreme societal unrest, and the upcoming election of the next President of the United States. To say there's a putrid stew of chaos, confusion, hate, and fear in our country is an understatement.

According to God's plan, I infused science into my training. I taught the gals about their unique fingerprints and extraordinarily specific DNA to encourage them not to compare. I prompted them to use their visual voice (speaking through what is seen, not heard) to paint their thoughts. I assured them that their voice was powerful because, according to the human genome, no other person existed like them. And then I asked the girls to close their eyes and imagine giving a gift to someone in this crazy season. "What would you give them?" I asked. "Would you give them hope, strength, courage, love, kindness, peace?" I continued to list off positive feelings and then asked them to choose one and paint it abstractly onto the canvas. "What does a feeling look like?" I asked rhetorically. "No one knows, so you can't get it wrong," I encouraged.

I thought the training went well. I would have preferred to do it in person rather than online, per Covid restrictions, but overall, it was good. I was encouraged by a few of the girls as they moved beyond their comfort zone and dared to share their paintings and their feelings about the process. Fairly satisfied with the results, I thanked God for what I witnessed and prayed that He would continue to bless them.

The next day, I received an email testimony from the coordinator that rocked me to the core and had me blubbering like a baby. Sobbing and speechless, I pointed my phone towards my husband and managed to whimper, "Read this." I watched and waited. With tears streaming down his face, my husband and partner in our creative ministry turned to me and whispered, "This is why we do what we do."

And this is why God does what He does through us.

After the training, one of the moms who was online with her daughter asked about what her painting represented. She explained that it was a message for a friend. As they continued the conversation, it took an unexpected and shocking turn when the daughter shared that this particular friend was planning to commit suicide. As she offloaded the great weight of the secret she had been carrying, both mother and child wept together and then called the other girl's mother. The result: The impending suicide was prevented, meaningful conversations took place, and they began the journey of healing and restoration.

A finger painting workshop saved the life of a 15-year-old girl.

This is one of many testimonies I've experienced about the Supernatural presence and power of God working through creative expression. And this is one of the many reasons God called me to write *Supernatural Creativity*. It's not enough for me to have these experiences; God is calling you to have them too. He is calling you to the front lines to collaborate with His Spirit and use your creative expression—no matter what it is—to advance His purposes.

If you're reading this book, consider yourself called.

Let's do this!
Jill Elizabeth Wyckoff

> *"I pray that the eyes of your heart may be enlightened, so that you will know what is the hope of His calling, what are the riches of the glory of His inheritance in the saints, what is the boundless greatness of His power toward us who believe."*
>
> — Ephesians 1:18, 19 (NASB)

Contents

Introduction xi

Section 1: Oh My God! 1

    Chapter 1: It All Starts Here 3

    Chapter 2: OMG & Me 11

    Chapter 3: So What Is It? 17

    Chapter 4: The Real You 27

    Chapter 5: Part Of The Plan 41

Section 2: Saying Yes 53

    Chapter 6: Partnering With The Power 55

    Chapter 7: The Power Of Choice 63

    Chapter 8: Humble Beginnings 69

    Chapter 9: The Rhythm Of The Spirit 75

    Chapter 10: The Creative Lifestyle 81

    Chapter 11: Obstacles To Obedience 91

    Chapter 12: Recess 105

    Chapter 13: Come As A Child 109

    Chapter 14: Just Imagine 111

    Chapter 15: Overcoming 119

    Chapter 16: To Be Or Not To Be 127

Section 3: The Call To Restorative Impact 129

    Chapter 17: God's Creative Army 131

    Chapter 18: Inside Out 137

    Chapter 19: Give It Up 145

    Chapter 20: Eyes To See And Ears To Hear 149

    Chapter 21: Community 157

Chapter 22: Collaboration 163

Chapter 23: Your Why, Who, & What 169

Chapter 24: Show & Tell 175

Section 4: Boots On The Ground 183

Chapter 25: Hide and Seek 185

Chapter 26: Permission Granted 189

Chapter 27: Stranger Than Fiction 193

Chapter 28: Testimonies 197

Section 5: Remember 213

Chapter 29: Who Am I? 215

Chapter 30: Who Is He? 219

Chapter 31: Protein Snack 223

Section 6: Released 233

Chapter 32: Success And Humility 235

Chapter 33: Commissioning 237

Afterword 241

Author's Bio 243

Section 1
Oh My God!

Chapter 1
It All Starts Here

TAKE A MOMENT to imagine a time before music and laughter; before fireflies and roly-polies; before puppies, poppies, mountains, meadows, and movies. Imagine a time before everything you've ever seen, heard, touched, smelled, and tasted. No history. Black. Void. Nothing.

"In the beginning, God created..." (Genesis 1:1) There was nothing. And then there was something. The first line of the Bible reveals the first thing God wants you to know about Himself. He is a creator. Actually, I take that back. He is THE Creator.

He could have described himself as the omnipotent force behind all that we see. He could have used descriptors like omniscient, omnipresent, and glorious—all very *God-like* characteristics. That's marketing 101, right? I mean, who wouldn't be attracted to a Being who is all-powerful, all-knowing, all-present, and full of glory? And if you're going to write a book of biblical proportions (literally), wouldn't you want to shock and awe your audience right out of the gate?

In actuality, He did.

God started the book of all books with a line so inconspicuous that it lands as gentle as a whisper. If we don't lean our ear towards it, we might miss it altogether. But for those with ears to hear, the first line of God's Word is mighty to change the trajectory of your life—if you allow it.

God, in His infinite wisdom, desires all His offspring first and foremost to understand that their Daddy is The Master Creator.

> *"For by Him all things were created, both in the heavens and on earth, visible and invisible, whether thrones, or dominions, or rulers, or authorities—all things have been created through Him and for Him."*
>
> — Colossians 1:16 (NASB)

You included.

You might be thinking, *Well, that's a given. Of course, He created me. I get it.* It sounds rudimentary to me as well. We all know that the Bible says somewhere in the beginning-ish that God said, Let us make man in our image and likeness (Gen 1:26). It's true that we can recite that line well enough to make our first grade Sunday school teacher blush with pride, but how many of us have really meditated on the enormity of it? We, us, puny in every way next to God, have been created and designed to bear His image and likeness. And He did it on purpose.

Once you let this absorb into your marrow, the way you think about yourself and your creative expression will shift. God wants you to truly know Him as Creator and yourself as His son or daughter. **You carry the genetic markings of the creator of EVERYTHING. In Genesis, God is very clear about His design, so you'll be very clear about yours.**

Just how creative is your Daddy God?

He said, "Let there be light," and BAM! There it was!

God breathed out light at 186,282 miles per second. Some believe He sang it into existence; an ethereal melodic resonance that birthed countless stars across innumerable galaxies. He placed planet Earth perfectly positioned amongst the 100+ billion stars in our own Milky Way galaxy; 93 million miles away from the sun; not too close, or we'd incinerate; not too far, or we'd freeze. Scientists call this fine-tuning; the constants and qualities of our universe that have to be *infinitesimally* precise to sustain life. I call it the act of a Master Creator who is Perfect Love.

Astronomers estimate that there are roughly two trillion galaxies in the known universe and around one billion trillion stars (that's a 1 with 21 zeros after it). To add to this, creation continues. Every second another star is born. You and I know from Genesis 1 who created all those stars. And we also know from reading Psalm 147 that The Creator must be very fond of them because He knows exactly how many there are, and He calls them all by name.

C.S. Lewis painted a wondrous picture of this epic creation event in *The Magician's Nephew (Harper Collins, 2008).*

> Then two wonders happened at the same moment. One was that the voice was suddenly joined by other voices; more voices than you could possibly count. They were in harmony with it, but far higher up the scale: cold, tingling, silvery voices. The second wonder was that the blackness overhead, all at once, was blazing with stars. They didn't come out gently one by one, as they do on a summer evening. One moment there had been nothing but darkness; next moment a thousand, thousand points of light leaped out—single stars, constellations, and planets, brighter and bigger than any in our world. There were no clouds. The new stars and the new voices began at exactly the same time. If you had seen and heard it, as Digory did, you would have felt quite certain that it was the stars themselves which were singing, and that it was the First Voice, the deep one, which had made them appear and made them sing.

Isaiah in the Bible paints his own picture of this when he implores us to behold the magnitude of the great and mighty God we serve :

> *"Raise your eyes on high and see who has created these stars, the One who brings out their multitude by number,*

He calls them all by name; because of the greatness of His might and the strength of His power, not one of them is missing."

— Isaiah 40:26 (NASB)

We cannot begin to fathom how big God is or how vast His imagination. I heard a preacher once say that the four living creatures in Revelation 4 *never* stop saying, "Holy, holy, holy is the Lord God Almighty, who was, and is, and is to come," because every time they look up at Him they discover another facet of who He is. God is *that* big.

As we continue on in Genesis 1, we discover more of God's imagination come to life on our planet. God created the creatures in the water, the birds in the sky, every kind of animal, and a plethora of creepy crawly things (Gen 1:20-25 grossly paraphrased). This is no less awe-inspiring than the stars, but when it comes to God's warm and cold-blooded creations, we see that He has a creative sense of humor.

Now, I must warn you that I have a penchant for looking stuff up online. Google—the tree of the knowledge of good and evil—as Pastor Nathalie Armstrong of Citadel Church in Seattle calls it, can unleash a world of fascinating information. It can also send you down Alice's rabbit hole. In no time at all, you'll find you've wasted a whole day with nothing to show for it but a sore bum and the faint feeling of a Cheshire cat grinning satisfactorily nearby. But in this case, I was able to dig up these fun little *"Are you kidding me?!"* kind of facts that make you shake your head and wonder at the creative genius of your Daddy God. He thinks these things up and then makes them out of nothing. He definitely thinks outside the box!

- Sea sponges have no head, mouth, eyes, feelers, bones, heart, lungs, or brain, yet they are alive. (*I should think about these the next time I'm lying around like a lifeless blob. No excuses!*)
- A shrimp's heart is in its head. (*Why? That's what I'm wondering. Hmmm...Does it think with his heart?*)
- An Octopus has three hearts, nine brains, and blue blood.

(*Nine brains! And we humans don't even use a fraction of the one we have. Maybe that's why God only gave us one.*)

- Dolphins sleep with only half of their brain and with one eye open so they can watch for predators and other threats. (*Watchdogs—Watch dolphins? Whodathunk?*)
- Slugs have 4 noses; two for detecting light, two for smelling. (*They may be sluggish, but they're well equipped.*)
- The ant can carry 5000 times its own weight (*I have trouble with two bags of groceries and a gallon of milk*).

Okay, if these facts haven't stupefied you and rendered you speechless, how about this?

The Golden Orb Spider releases spider silk that is, pound for pound, five times stronger than steel. It has been said that, due to its amazing strength and elasticity, you could trap a jumbo jet with this spider's silk that is the thickness of a pencil. I, for one, am freaked out by spiders; but maybe this little guy is the genius behind Spiderman. Who knows?

And then there's the Bar-Tailed Godwit—Love this sweet birdie!

Scientists tracked a Godwit, a little bird weighing less than one pound, to discover that it flew 7,145 miles in nine days without stopping, averaging 34.8 mph. This little guy flew over 16,000 miles (roundtrip) without taking a break to eat, drink, rest, or nest. If that isn't astounding enough, he ended up exactly where he began (internal GPS?). Godwits can fly tens of thousands of miles without ever getting lost. My husband likes to joke that if I stood in the driveway, closed my eyes, and turned around in a circle a couple of times, I wouldn't be able to find my way home. Unlike the Godwit, I have a bit of a challenge when it comes to directions. But I digress.

I know these incredible facts are a lot to absorb, but they're kind of fun, so I'll add one more:

Every year, scientists find new species. To date, a total of 1.3 million species have been identified and described. Currently, scientists estimate more than 8.7 million species live on the planet, but they really don't know. How could they? God is currently creating new ones.

Suffice it to say that our Father God's creativity goes far beyond our 3-pound brain's ability to comprehend. But try to imagine this: Everything God created, He created for us; day, night, earth, sky, water, plants, every living thing—all of it good, all of it from nothing, and all of it for us. Why? Because *we* are His greatest creation!

Explore Some More:

- Check out Louie Giglio videos about our universe on YouTube.
- After researching Giglio, read Genesis 1 and see if it takes on a whole new dimension.

Chapter 2
OMG & Me

EVEN THOUGH WE'VE barely scratched the surface, it's pretty eye-opening to consider how masterfully creative our Papa God is. It's times like these when words just don't cut it, which makes it difficult when writing a book. I'm sitting here at my computer shaking my head in awe. Everything about Him utterly astounds me. But here's the thing, if we don't take the time to see God as He is and meditate on His magnificence, we will start to forget. When this happens, we make the mistake of making Him small enough to fit within our limited knowledge and understanding—we mold Him into our own image and likeness. We cannot imagine God greater than our experience of Him, which in turn, limits our experience of Him.

As we set off on our Supernatural creative journey, we need to remind ourselves over and over again of the One who created us to create.

You probably surmised that I love to use science as a way of pointing to the majesty and splendor of God. This field of study works whether you're speaking with Christian or secular (pre-Christian) audiences. People think science and religion don't mix. I wholeheartedly disagree. I have found that besides the Word of God and personal experience, it's the most effective way to reveal the nature of God. So let's keep rolling with that.

Ladies and gentlemen, prepare to be awed and inspired by the result of your Daddy God's creative masterpiece—His *pièce de ré·sis·tance*—His poem in motion—YOU!

You were created when 1 cell from your dad hooked up with 1 cell from your mom. Each cell carrying 23 pairs of chromosomes matched up—a feat in itself—and eventually grew into the 100 trillion cells in your body. Snug and cozy inside each of these cells lie the 3 billion characters that make up your DNA code—the story of you. To give you a perspective of how brilliantly specific your story, if your DNA was put end to end, it would reach the sun and back over 600 times (93 million miles away, for a total of 55 billion, 800 million miles).

Some of us have always felt different, like we're not like everyone else. That's because we're not. There never has been nor ever will be anyone on the planet who is exactly like you—this is by intentional design—our DNA confirms it.

Some of you might be thinking, "Sure, I know we're different. Look at our fingerprints." I agree. Our fingerprints are an obvious sign. But it takes it up a notch (or billions of notches) to look deeper and try to wrap our minds around the fact that we're 55 billion, 800 million miles worth of different? God really took His time imagining you. He intricately crafted your story with the utmost care and precision. He wants you to know how very special you are.

> *"I will give thanks to You, because I am awesomely and wonderfully made; wonderful are Your works, and my soul knows it very well."*
>
> — Psalm 139:14 (NASB)

> *"The womb is God's art studio."*
>
> — Lou Engle

Did you know that your brain is composed of 80 percent water and can hold five times as much information as the Encyclopedia Britannica, or that your eyes can distinguish up to one million color surfaces and take in more information than the largest existing telescope? You probably haven't thought much about your liver, but it works over 400 functions in your body. It's such an incredible work of creative genius that if two-thirds were removed it could grow back to its original size in four weeks.

You are a sign and a wonder!

St Augustine said, "Men go abroad to wonder at the heights of mountains, at the huge waves of the sea, at the long courses of the rivers, at the vast compass of the ocean, at the circular motions of the stars, and they pass by themselves without wondering."

God is calling us to pay attention to the intricacies of our design and the magnitude of our Designer.

When my grandson, Avery, was 4 years old, he had the following conversation with his mother (my eldest daughter). This simple, yet profoundly beautiful exchange, captures the essence of God's creative process. It is as pure and unpretentious as the child himself—its innocence and matter-of-factness revealing an understanding well beyond his years.

Avery, "How did God make us?"

Mom, "He breathed life into each of us."

Avery, "He used his imagination."

Mom, "Yes, and He made us in his own image."

Avery, "He painted us."

God imagined you and painted you into being. You are His exquisite masterpiece.

Try This:

- Do an online search of the wonders of the human body and be awed by your design and your Designer.
- Start a conversation with someone using at least one of these facts to encourage them in their specific design.
- Take note of how this conversation made the individual feel and how it made you feel.

What if things
didn't look
quite like
you thought
they did...
    or should?

Just imagine.

Chapter 3
So What Is It?

"Creativity is contagious, pass it on."

—Albert Einstein

"Imagination is the beginning of creation. You imagine what you desire, you will what you imagine, and at last, you create what you will."

— George Bernard Shaw

N THIS CHAPTER, I will attempt to (1) expand your vision of what creativity is in its natural expression and (2) provide an explanation of what creativity is as a Supernatural expression.

In The Natural

Ask ten people what creativity is, and you're likely to get ten different answers. Here are a few creative answers by those in the know:

"Creativity is intelligence having fun."

— Albert Einstein

"Creativity is a wild mind and a disciplined eye."
— Dorothy Parker

"Creativity is the way I share my soul with the world."
— Brene Brown

"Creativity is inventing, experimenting, growing, taking risks, breaking rules, making mistakes, and having fun."
— Mary Lou Cook

"Creativity is taking your imagination out for a walk."
— Jill Wyckoff

Merriam-Webster online dictionary defines creativity simply as (1) the ability to create, and (2) the quality of being creative. *Dictionary. com* defines creativity as, "(1) The state or quality of being creative, (2) The ability to transcend traditional ideas, rules, patterns, relationships, or the like, and to create meaningful new ideas, forms, methods, interpretations, etc; originality, progressiveness, or imagination, and (3) The process by which one utilizes creative ability." All of these descriptions are correct, and yet, none in itself is complete.

We are challenged by the lines we've erected to box in our definition of creativity. With our own limited interpretation neatly confined within these lines, we can comfortably risk nothing and excuse or disqualify ourselves at any given moment. "I don't have a creative bone in my body," we say—half hoping it's not really true and half convinced that it is. How many of us think that creativity is only expressed as the books we read, the shows we binge-watch, the music we dance to, and the paintings on our walls? We think to ourselves, "Those are created by the 'really' creative people—the true artists." But what if you're not a classically trained artist in one of those disciplines? Does that disqualify you from being creative?

Only you can disqualify you from being creative. Here's the

reality—If you're breathing, you're creative. Why? Because you take after your Father God.

If you've ever cooked a meal, frosted a cake, taught a child, made a spreadsheet, sewed a button, written a poem, fixed your car, decorated your apartment, organized your closet, started a business, planned a budget, picked out a great outfit, bought the perfect gift for a friend (on sale!), developed a service, made up a joke, had an idea to make something better, talked your way out of (or into) anything, you're creative! In fact, most people probably have no idea just how creative they are.

Right here, right now, before we move on, I pray that you will recognize the big picture. See yourself and everything around you as the fruit of someone's imagination. First, God's imagination, then people's. Everything that exists, be it a product, an idea, a structure, a system, exists because someone imagined it. And the greatest things that exist are because God imagined them. You are His greatest creation—He imagined you—His image in you. You have the ability to create because He first created.

Next time you brush your teeth, think about who created the toothbrush with its pokey little bristles and who created the toothpaste with its minty fresh flavor. Next time you walk into the bank, think about who created the banking system, the money counting machines, the cash and the coins. There are many things in our everyday life that we do not associate with creative expression.

What is Creativity? I've taken my imagination out for a walk, and this is what I came up with:

Creativity defines beauty, defies beauty, reveals truth and tells lies.
It can be haunting, heinous, gaudy, glorious,
Nouveau, Deco, Draconian, Renaissance.
Video, virtual, digital, technical,
spectacle, theatrical, and oft times unethical.
Inventions, collaboration, decoration, playstation,
strategizing, organizing, innovating, figure skating,

baking, graffiti, graphics, and Gaga,
garage bands, wedding bands, Band of Brothers, Brothers Grimm,
Right Said Fred, Drop Dead Fred, The Walking Dead, and Talking
Heads
Street art, pop art, Pop-Tarts...think about it
political, satirical, historical, and lyrical.
Sewing, writing, poetry, pour-overs,
sculpture, architecture, techno, and don't ya know...
even Velvet Elvis and dogs playing poker.
Snoopy, Snoop Dog, Spiderman, Green Eggs & Ham,
Hamilton, Catcher in the Rye, pastrami on rye (yummm),
comedy, tragedy, Times Square and Broadway,
Talk shows, HBO, ShowTime, show tunes,
Tomorrowland, Land's End, Land Before Time, Busta Rhymes.
Typography, choreography, memes, and biographies,
house painting, figure painting, finger painting, campaigning,
drawing, dancing, do-si-do's and do re mi's,
even dohickeys involve creativity.
Creativity is thought-provoking, challenging and poking, in your
face,
facelift, face makeup, skincare, hair out to there,
tattoos, Moody blues, Blue like Jazz, RagTime
jewelry, Jetsons, jingles, and Pringles,
(once you pop, you just can't stop).
Marketing, mashups, monuments, and mani-pedis,
Mona Lisa, Madonna, Mary Mary quite contrary.
Clothing, fashion, Givenchy, Juicy,
Coco Chanel. Hello! Did someone say cocoa?
Ghirardelli, incredible edibles,
now that's creativity you can sink your teeth into—

tasty creations that please the palate.

Pallet planters, pallet coffee tables, pallet bookshelves, pallet everything!

Pinterest!

Creativity is culture-shaping, ever-changing. It's here, it's there, it's everywhere

Even Jesus was a carpenter.

Creativity fills our senses but isn't always sensible and is most often insensitive to the ways of the Spirit.

And so it needs us to rise above the fray

And make a new way for Jesus to have his say,

not just in a galaxy far, far away,

But here on earth as it is in heaven.

Because "That's the way, uh huh, uh huh, I like it, uh huh, uh huh."

Ya know, even YOU are God's creative expression.

You are God's poema. His poem.

His symphony. His happy melody.

You're meant to be

seen...heard...valued.

You're designed to express beauty and light, provoke thought, incite justice,

initiate conversation, change worldviews, build bridges, and transform cultures.

You were created to show the world life as it should be.

You are God's creative masterpiece.

Supernatural Creativity

"Supernatural: of or relating to an order of existence beyond the visible observable universe *especially* of or relating to God or a god, demigod, spirit, or devil: departing from what is usual or normal especially so as to appear to transcend the laws of nature" (Merriam-Webster).

What is Supernatural creativity? For Kingdom purposes, it is any creative expression under the influence of the Holy Spirit that reveals the nature of God expressed through a collaboration of Spirit and man. Its transformative quality is limitless because God is limitless. As such, it has the power to make a restorative impact on an individual or societal level.

"Restorative: something that serves to restore to consciousness, vigor, or health" (Merriam-Webster).

God's consciousness, vigor, and health are beyond anything we can obtain in this natural world. It is a return to original design, before the fall. We all know there's no going back. We cannot turn back the pages of time and restore what was stolen and/or given up in the Garden of Eden. Knowing this, God made a way through His son, Jesus Christ. He is the way, the truth, and the life. When we surrender our lives to Him, we take hold of His righteousness—life as it should be. **As the redeemed of the Lord, we carry His Holy Spirit. We've always had the ability to create because we bear the image of our Papa God. Our salvation gives us access and authority to collaborate with the Holy Spirit and release more than just pretty things and good ideas. Our creative expressions are infused with the manifest power and presence of God to reveal His nature. This is Supernatural creativity.**

I've learned not to underestimate it.

I had no idea I could paint a prayer and God could answer it.

As you'll discover in the next chapter, I am a finger painter. I will share with you my creative journey, but for now, suffice it to say that it started with little to no faith in my own ability nor in God's ability to work through me. But God was ever patient in His encouragement, gentle in His prodding, and faithful to snap me out of it!

Near the beginning of my journey, in the midst of my process, God encountered me in a way I will never forget. I was happily preparing to paint on a beautifully sunny day in Southern California, where I live.

The birds were singing cheerful melodies; a gentle breeze was blowing through the Pepper tree leaves. Conditions were idyllic. Suddenly, I felt an overwhelming urge to paint darkness. It went against everything I was feeling at the time, but it was so strong that I gave in and swished my hand through the black paint. As I slapped the paint across the canvas, I got the impression of a title—Out of the Ashes. Up until that point, I had not titled my paintings because I felt that to do so was to limit the viewers' experience and personal interpretation. I continued to paint, and I got another impression. Pray for Joe (not his real name). *Hell no*! I thought. He was the last person on earth I wanted to pray for! Joe had done unthinkable harm to my family, and he could rot, for all I cared. I know this sounds harsh and certainly not what Jesus would think, but it was how I felt at the time. I literally froze, mid paint stroke, with absolute incredulity. I couldn't believe what God was asking me to do.

"God, how can I do this? You know what he did."

"Yes, I know, but I want you to pray for him."

"God, I don't even know what to pray. I don't have the words."

"That's ok. Paint it. Paint your prayer."

And so I did. Not necessarily willingly, but out of obedience. God had given me a title, so that's what I painted—*Out of the Ashes*. I painted a spot of light in the midst of the darkness; a tiny splotch of a green shoot poking out of the soot. It was my unspoken painted prayer. And I hung it up on the wall to remind myself. As time passed, it got easier to walk by it and throw up a little prayer for Joe. I felt my heart shifting. I could almost believe that Joe could change.

I don't remember exactly how long it was, but it was probably close to a year later when Joe returned to our lives. Transformation had begun to take place—not completely, but there was a definite difference. In one of those beautiful Divine set-ups God loves to pull off, He orchestrated for us to meet and for me to gift him the painting. I explained to Joe that God led me to paint a prayer for him, and I believed that he was starting to walk out the manifestation of this answered prayer. This painting, I explained, revealed how God saw him; with potential and promise for rebirth as His child—a new creation—the former sin washed away by the blood of Jesus.

I found out later that he sat in the car for over an hour, weeping over his painting as he experienced the love of His Father.

It's true; I had no idea I could paint a prayer. Little did I know then that in my obedience, the Holy Spirit would work with me and through me to paint a prophecy. Through this simple 16 x 20 finger painting, empowered by the Spirit of God, I would witness the manifestation of the title He gave me—*Out of the Ashes.*

> *"Whatever you create out of an experience with God becomes an invitation or a doorway to that experience. Artisans are being called as a secret weapon to astound the world with the sounds, sights, and smells of heaven."*
>
> — Bill Johnson

This is the power of Supernatural creativity. I have since witnessed hundreds of testimonies of God's restorative impact through creative expression. I've seen people saved, healed, and delivered through paintings, poems, books, and baked goods. I will share some of these testimonies in later chapters.

Now that you know Supernatural creativity exists, there are two very important things to remember. First, God works His power through all creative expressions, not just the traditional arts. If you try to put Him in a box, He will burst through it every time. And second, if you let Him, He will work through YOU. To believe anything less would be a sad case of mistaken identity about God and about yourself.

Write it Down:

- What are some of the new ideas you have about creativity now that you didn't have before?
- What are the areas of creative expression that draw you? Make a list without thinking about whether or not you have any ability in those areas.

Chapter 4
The Real You

AM A FINGER painter. I paint with my hands because I don't know how to use brushes. I am not traditionally trained in finger painting or anything else for that matter. I started painting about eight years ago. I fell in love with the feel of wet paint on my hands, and I discovered that I could paint what I felt, not necessarily what I saw. I would dance my hands across the canvas to the rhythm of the worship music blasting in the background and end up with something abstractly beautiful. It was, and is, my out of the box expression; no agendas, no performance, just blissful freedom.

In that first year, I painted a number of paintings. My friend (I'll call her Ann) called me prolific. I'd never been called that before. I had to look it up just to make sure it meant what I thought it meant. Ann told other friends about my paintings and encouraged me to show them. Flattered but embarrassed, I would disqualify myself. *Oh, I'm just a finger painter,* I thought. God forbid they would have a high expectation and I would fail to deliver.

Around that time, Ann (ever the encourager) went with me to a bric-a-brac type shop that offered art classes. We thought maybe they would allow me to rent space and offer my own classes there. With Ann by my side for moral support, I explained to the shop owner that I was just a finger painter, but I thought people would like to experience the freedom of that style of painting. In the end, her rental prices were beyond my budget. But I will never forget that day because of the conversation Ann and I had when we left the shop.

Ann. "You have to stop saying that."

Me. "Saying what?"

Ann. "Stop saying you're just a finger painter."

Me. "Why? That's what I am."

Ann. "No. You're not just a finger painter. You're an artist."

She was very firm, but also rather matter of fact. Like, Doy, don't you get it?! It was at that moment, unbeknownst to her, God used my beautiful agnostic friend to set me on a new course. I knew He was purposely moving me beyond my comfort zone. He had a plan for me, and if I was going to walk it out, I had to accept the way He saw me and not be content with the way I saw myself.

It wasn't easy. Whenever I called myself an artist, it was like waving a sign and shouting into a megaphone, "Everyone, look at me, I'm a big fat liar!" I pictured people laughing at me, mocking me for the no-talent wannabe that I was. I felt boastful and ugly. "I am an artist." Shrink, shrink, gag, gag, liar-liar pants on fire. It was so much easier to think of myself as "just a finger painter." But there are no "easy" buttons in our walk with God. I had to press through the difficulties; step into His truth. My breakthrough came as a result of my obedience. I believe this is true for all of us.

In time, it became more comfortable and started to roll off my lips without burning them. Eventually, it became part of me. God says it, so I believe it. "I am an artist." This is not to say that I don't slide a little bit backwards on occasion, especially when I'm listening to my favorite podcast, *Makers & Mystics*. "Now these are REAL artists," I think to myself, and it feels like a slap to my face with my very own hand. But these days, I'm able to rally before the sting starts to set in. It's a wake-up call, really. I know that the enemy of my soul is messing with my mind. (I've got a lot more to say on this subject later in the book).

Okay, so I'm an artist. Good for me, right? You, on the other hand, may not be there yet. That's quite alright. I shared this story mainly as an example of how God transforms our minds. He did it with me, and He will do it with you if you say yes and move forward with Him, despite the awkwardness.

> *"Embracing what God does for you is the best thing you can do for him. Don't become so well-adjusted to your culture that you fit into it without even thinking. Instead, fix your attention on God. You'll be changed from the inside out. Readily recognize what he wants from you, and quickly respond to it. Unlike the culture around you, always dragging you down to its level of immaturity, God brings the best out of you, develops well-formed maturity in you."*
>
> — Romans 12 1-2 (MSG)

Moving from immaturity to maturity is the natural progression of the Christian life. This is the reason you're reading this book; to mature in your beautiful God-given design; to advance in His calling for you as a Kingdom creative. You don't have to call yourself an artist if God isn't asking you to do so. For you to progress, however, you must embrace and acknowledge that God has a specific and intentional plan for you. **He placed His creative nature *in* you to reveal Himself *through* you.** Write this on your heart and let it sink into your bones—you have what it takes—you've had it all along.

> *"Before I formed you in the womb I knew you, and before you were born I consecrated you;"*
>
> — Jeremiah 1:5 (NASB)

When I was a little girl, my mom and dad thought I had talent. They used to hang my pictures on the fridge and brag about me to their friends. "Look at the brilliant picture my little Jill painted. Isn't it beautiful?!" Whenever they had company, my mom would shout from the living room, "Jill, bring your guitar and sing a song for everyone!"

Embarrassed, I would clumsily strum the chords, trying desperately not to mess up, while haltingly singing—Red River Vaaaaalley (halt for chord change, take a breath) the valley so (chord change, breath) looooow. My parents and their friends would applaud as if I was the headliner at the Grand Ole Opry. I was treated like I was nothing short of a creative genius, and I started to believe it. And because I started to believe it, I kept it up.

By the time I hit high school, my creativity had become more about me than pleasing my parents; an outward expression of my inward emotions—teenage angst. I loved all forms of creativity; holding up in my bedroom for hours on end, drawing, painting, singing, and writing. Locked away from the chaos of my large family, I could create the world I wanted to live in, which, by the way, was vastly different from the reality of the world I actually did live in. Creativity was my lifeline—it was the best part of me—it was my bliss. I dreamed of growing up and working in a creative field. And then I graduated high school, and something inside my very creative brain snapped.

> *"Every child is an artist. The problem is how to remain an artist once we grow up."*
>
> — Pablo Picasso

While I was closed off from the rest of the world safely tucked away in the sanctuary of my room (no internet), I could create without limits, without risk. I could even imagine that I was quite good at it. After all, according to my mom and dad, I was a flippin' creative genius. But when I opened the door to what lay beyond the harbor of my home, I was sucker-punched with the cold hard reality of the lie I'd been living. The truth was that compared to others, I sucked.

"To my mother, I'm an artist. To my father, I'm an artist. To an artist, I'm noooo artist!" I would mock dramatically in a thick New York Jewish accent, mimicking my mother's Yiddish schtick records. I pretended it was funny. But it wasn't. To my way of thinking, it was the truth.

And so, with comparison as my excuse, I gave up my creative expressions one by one. With the exception of eventually singing to my young children or every now and then in the shower, I discredited and stuffed away everything else.

A funny thing happens when you try to hide your true original design. It leaks out little by little. You find yourself in jobs where they need a creative solution to a problem and *voila!*—your idea is perfect. Or a friend needs a name for their new business, and wouldn't you know it, you've got it! Oh, and you've got the tagline and the logo too. It seeps out of you in a million different ways that you're not even aware of. You think of a great way to entertain your kids during the 10-hour drive to Grandma's. You make their Halloween costumes. You create the perfect Italian meal without a recipe. You imagine an alternate ending to a movie. You create the church bulletin or the company newsletter. You get an idea for a book you think someone should write. You think of a better way of doing something. You write a speech for your boss or create the perfect spreadsheet. You invent things in your head. The list goes on and on. It is impossible to turn off what God turned on inside of you. No matter how hard you try, "You can run, but you can't hide."

January 4, 2009, my husband, Brae, and I walked into The Awakening Church in Carlsbad, CA. We had given our lives to Jesus a number of years prior, had a few church experiences, but had stopped going for almost two years. We weren't backslidden or angry at God. We just felt that something was missing, but couldn't figure out what. We tried a variety of churches during this time but felt like they were sucking the life out of God and out of us. On December 26, 2008, we met up with friends we hadn't seen in a long while, and they suggested The Awakening. We attended a week later and began an 11-year period of discovery that would change the trajectory of our lives.

That first Sunday, we knew we wanted to come back. In short order, we discovered what was missing. It was the third person of the

Trinity—The Holy Spirit of God. Even though Brae and I were both saved, neither of us had grown up in a traditional Christian church home. Brae's folks were homegrown to the bone Woodstock hippies. They believed that all roads lead to heaven and had pictures of Budha, yogis, and Jesus on their mantle. I was raised in Christian Science, a metaphysical religion founded by a woman named Mary Baker Eddy, which teaches that there is no such thing as sin. I never heard about the Holy Spirit except in reference to the ghost my Catholic friends prayed to. The Christian churches we attended prior to The Awakening were seeker-friendly and didn't have much to say on the subject. I believe there are churches for everyone no matter where they are in their spiritual journey, but for us, we will always be grateful that God led us to a church that taught the full expression of our Trinitarian God. It was the piece of the puzzle that was missing for us. It was the Power that testified to the Word and enabled us to live it and experience it. With God—the Father, Son, *and* Spirit—we discovered a whole new world of possibilities and purpose. It was life-changing.

I was awakened to the reality of *me*. Without going into great depths about my back story (you can read about it in my book, *Once Upon a Backpack*, available on Amazon), suffice it to say my life had been no great picnic. I had experienced molestation, murder, drugs, divorce, depression, and one devastating loss after another. My poor choices perpetuated my circumstances and left me living a shadow of the life I was meant to live. I was wracked with shame, guilt, and self-loathing. Thank God, He never gave up on me. He dropped Divine bread crumbs along my path that led me to His outstretched arms, patiently beckoning me to draw nearer to the truth that would set me free.

As I learned more about God, I discovered more about myself. And as I stepped into the Truth of His Word and the Power of His Spirit, things started happening—wonderful, strange, Supernatural type things. Even more incredible than what was going on around me was what was happening within me. Little by little, I sought Him more boldly. As I embarked on the journey with intentionality, I was healed of unforgiveness towards others, and even more difficult, of the unforgiveness I held towards myself. It didn't happen overnight. But I charted a steady course of going after the things of God, and despite my circumstances, I stuck with it.

This is the point where I ever so slightly cracked open the door to creativity. Of course, I see now that it was a Divine set-up. You know about those, right?

I tried painting and immediately felt frustrated. Hard as I tried, I couldn't make my paintings look as good as other people's. So I stopped trying. As quickly as I had cracked the door open, I shut it. Why bother?!

Then one day I went to a friend's house, and she told me about finger painting. She was in the backyard making a mess, paint splattered everywhere, her curly blonde locks bouncing as she excitedly told me about this new thing she was trying out. She had just come from a visit with her father, an accomplished artist. After complaining that she couldn't do what he could do, he suggested she try painting with her hands. She was thrilled at this new discovery and the serendipitous results that were beyond her expectations. I watched and learned.

I was 52 years old when I started finger painting. I often say (half-jokingly) that finger painting changed my life. Of course, I know that the reality is that God changed my life, but He definitely used finger painting as a tool.

I started painting every day. I loved standing in front of a blank canvas with worship music blasting the beat that would set my hands in motion on the canvas. I had no thought for the finish line. No agenda. If I heard God whisper blue, I'd paint blue. If I had a thought to paint a wiggly line, I'd paint a wiggly line. It was pure joy. I felt God's pleasure in my freedom to express without preconceptions or expectations. Even as I write about it now, I get a feeling of absolute delight.

God let me play by myself for a while. We were having fun together, and I didn't think it would ever be more than that. But God always has more. He gracefully gave me the choice to step into the new thing or stay where I was. If I stayed put, I would continue to enjoy the act of painting. It would be like what I had done as a teen, creating from the safety of my own space. no prying eyes, no chance of ridicule. But if I responded to God and risked moving forward, what would I discover? What more could God possibly have for little ol' me?

> "*Now to Him who is able to do far more abundantly beyond all that we ask or think, according to the power that works within us*"
>
> — Ephesians 3:20 (NASB)

God always has more for us than we can dream of, and He's given us everything we need to accomplish it. One of the biggest mistakes you or I can make is to believe that God cannot use little ol' us.

My friend, Henry Haney, a local worship leader, asked me to paint at his 24-hour worship event. He had seen my paintings at the house and wanted to include this artistic expression as a form of worship at his event. His request came prior to my conversation with Ann (mentioned previously), so my response was, "*Are you kidding? I'm just a finger painter. There's no way I'm ever going to paint in public. I don't do anything in front of people. People scare me!*"

Looking back now, I think God got a good chuckle out of that.

My friend kept pestering me, the Holy Spirit kept nudging me, and after arguing with God for a bit, I finally gave in. I was scared out of my wits, but I did it anyway. I tried to take the path of least resistance by calculating the time that I thought might pose the least risk. I suspected that, between 2 AM and 4 AM, there would be fewer people. So that's the time slot I chose to paint. Instead of using an easel where my work would be propped up for prying eyes, I placed the canvas on a table in the darkest back corner and hunkered over it like a squirrel protecting its last nut—and maybe it was nuts, but I couldn't help myself. Eventually, I was discovered and people started talking to me about my paintings. To my great surprise, these people were not scary. In fact, they were kind. In my head I had imagined all manner of responses: mocking, pointing, laughing, scoffing, but not kindness. Even more incredulous was that several people told me they had visions or dreams of my abstract paintings. This was the first inkling that God could do something Supernatural through my work. It was absolutely crazy, scary as hell, and extremely exciting all at the same time.

That night was the beginning of many new opportunities. Even though I was afraid, I agreed to say yes to whatever God wanted. And He honored that. He started opening more doors to paint in public: churches, beaches, even breweries. I walked through timidly at first. But as I grew to understand Him on a deeper level, I became more and more comfortable. In this part of the journey, He taught me about my fingerprints. He used science, as I relayed in Chapter 2, to help me understand the uniqueness of my design. The spirit-killer of comparison which had silenced my creative voice for years, was unmasked and revealed for the sham that it was. Just as no two fingerprints are alike, no two leaves, no two snowflakes, no two trees; no two people are alike and therefore they cannot create the same thing in the same way. It's utterly impossible—diversity is in our design.

I once heard Pastor Bill Johnson from Bethel Church in Redding, California say, "No one can do what you can do." It was early on in my awakening and I thought, "That's a bunch of crap. Anyone can do what I can do. I'm just a finger painter for gosh sake!" But when God started talking to me about my design, I realized Pastor Bill was right. God designed each of us to reveal a very specific part of His heart. If we give in to the lie of comparison, then the part of His heart that only we can reveal will never get seen or experienced on the face of the earth. That is a weighty revelation.

I love to see the look on my students' faces as they grasp the reality of that. To give an example, I talk about the very popular Paint and Palate events that have cropped up all over the nation. In your neck of the woods, they may be called Paint and Sip, or something clever like that, but the idea is to gather people together to paint, eat, and drink. In these events, 30-35 people are stationed at tables with their own canvas and materials. The artist shows them a sample of the painting they will paint and takes them, brushstroke by brushstroke through the steps. The paint is measured precisely. The brushes are color-coded. The teacher guides students to the exact spot where the paint brush is supposed to start and stop on the canvas instructing them (

amount of paint, pressure, and thickness of the stroke. It's a carefully crafted show-and-tell experience that takes a person of any artistic ability from zero to hero as their blank canvas emerges to look like that of the leader. And they do. But they also don't. Because they can't.

At the end of the night, when 35 students proudly hold up their paintings, you will see that they all look similar. But there are no two alike. Even if everyone follows the directions to the tee, there are always differences. You see, it has never been about being like someone else; it has always been about being different.

But why? Why did God take all the trouble to make my 55 billion, 800 million miles of DNA different than yours and the rest of humanity?

> "For we are His workmanship, created in Christ Jesus for good works, which God prepared beforehand so that we would walk in them."
> — Ephesians 2:10 (NIASB)

You and I are God's handiwork, the work of His hands. He created us purposely to do good works—not just any good works, but very specific works that He prepared and ordained for each of us to do. He purposely wrote this into our DNA and gave us the grace and ability to accomplish it by the blood of Jesus and the power of the Holy Spirit. And here's something you might want to consider: **It has nothing to do with what we produce. It's all about what God can produce through us.**

Our creative expression is a collaboration—us and Him—perfect partnership. It's not all on you, but it does take all of you. Once you truly accept what God says about your calling and what He says about you, a shift will take place, and transformation will begin. You will see yourself as a creative and step into God's version of you, which, by the way, is your original design. **It's not about *becoming* someone new. It's about *discovering* who you were always designed to be.**

My former pastor, Craig Muster, used to say, "If your view differs from God's view, then one of you is wrong, and it's not Him."

Dare to Believe:

- Ask God to show you anywhere you have a different view of yourself than His.
- Write these false beliefs down, and then write the truth of what God says about each one.

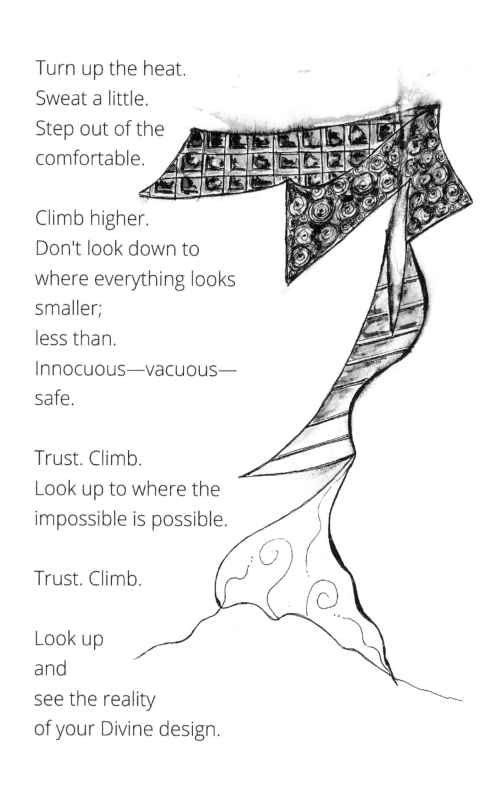

Turn up the heat.
Sweat a little.
Step out of the
comfortable.

Climb higher.
Don't look down to
where everything looks
smaller;
less than.
Innocuous—vacuous—
safe.

Trust. Climb.
Look up to where the
impossible is possible.

Trust. Climb.

Look up
and
see the reality
of your Divine design.

Chapter 5
Part Of The Plan

"There is a vitality, a life force, an energy, a quickening that is translated through you into action, and because there is only one of you in all time, this expression is unique. And if you block it, it will never exist through any other medium and will be lost."

— Martha Graham

'VE HAD THE pleasure of speaking at several of our Kingdom Creativity conferences here in San Diego. At one of the Q&A sessions, someone asked the panel, "What has been the biggest roadblock you've had to face in getting to where you are now?" Normally, I hold back a bit and give room for someone else to speak, but I jumped at this one. It was a no-brainer. "Without a doubt, the biggest roadblock I've had to face is me. I had to get out of my own way." The audience murmured agreement, the other panelists nodded knowingly.

In one way or another, we all have to get over ourselves. **We must let go of any belief that does not line up with what God says about us, or we will either paralyze ourselves into inactivity, move in a direction that is not God's best for us, or tread a weird combination of both that has us starting and stopping but never getting anywhere.**

Your beliefs dictate your action. If you believe God's word, you will offload your pre-Christ old dead man beliefs and inhabit your new-creation self. You will pursue His truth and His path. I'm not saying there won't be challenges along the way. There undoubtedly will. But from this solid foundation, you will be able to rise above the challenges and keep moving forward. It's imperative that you do because the whole world is groaning to see what God looks like through you.

Why? Because YOU are part of His Master plan!

> *"For I know the plans that I have for you,' declares the*
> *Lord, 'plans for prosperity and not for disaster, to give you*
> *a future and a hope'"*
> — Jeremiah 29:11 (NASB)

Most of us know this passage, but if you're like me you tend to focus on the latter part. Hallelujah—good plans, prosperous, no harm—yes! I can't tell you how many times I've recited this verse to give me hope when things looked hopeless. It's a beautiful reminder of the goodness of God who cares about His children and keeps His promises.

More recently, God highlighted something different in this scripture. It's not just that He has good plans for us; it's the fact that He has any plans at all—He has plans that involve us! The Master Creator of the entire universe (known and unknown) has a plan to allow you and me to manifest His will on earth as it is in heaven. According to Ephesians 2:10, it's very specific for each individual and already written into our design. It's pretty much a done deal. Except you have to walk it out.

How do we do that? I think of it in terms of the 5 R's. Recognize. Respond. Rely. Reveal. Represent. Let me explain…

Recognize

The first four chapters of this book were meant to lead you on a path of discovery and recognition. As this book is geared towards creatives,

I started out by explaining how creative God is and how creative you are as His son or daughter—a chip off the old block, as they say. Then I clarified that creativity is vast in its expression, so you'll start thinking outside the box. And it is Supernatural to bring restoration and transformation when you collaborate with the Holy Spirit. From there, we hit the hard stuff—the *real* you as opposed to *your version* of you. I shared my story because (a) it's real life, (b) you've probably felt similar feelings or had similar experiences, and (c) it shows the progression from unbelieving to believing—what my life was like when I believed my erroneous view of myself, and the transformation that occurred when I recognized the truth.

In the first four chapters, I attempted to lay a foundation that would reveal the absolute magnitude of God and His masterpiece—you. My prayer is that this book will lead you to dig deeper and pursue transformation. **Breakthrough begins with recognizing that God is your Master Creator and what He says about you is true.**

Respond

Once we recognize the truth, we have the choice to respond or not. As you know, God is a gentleman. He stands at the door and knocks. He doesn't barge in. He waits for us to exercise our free will to open the door. If we take that faith step, He will come in, hang out, be our best friend and biggest cheerleader. But we have to open the dang door.

Our response requires putting our beliefs into action, not just lip service. The Bible says that God puts His Spirit in us to "*move*" us (Ezekiel 36:27). He's waiting for us to move.

Rely

The first few times you move, you may be scared out of your wits like I was. In the beginning, I was seriously sick to my stomach every time I had to do anything in public. I worried that I would forget to breathe or poop my pants. TMI, but true. Regardless, I kept at it. I did it afraid, but I did it anyway. Why? Because deep down, I believed God would show up. And He did. He showed up the first time and every time. I didn't have to rely on my own strength or lack of it. I didn't have to count on my talent, my gifting, my anything. I just had to show up, fully present, willing to be a vessel for Him.

When we rely completely on God, He will never let us down. That's how it gets easier. We do it together—100% Him, 100% us— and He does all the heavy lifting.

It's true. It got easier and easier to stretch out of my comfort zone because of His faithfulness. And believe it or not, the unthinkable happened. Speaking in public, teaching, and preaching actually became my bliss. But take note, I don't stop relying on God now that it's easier. I still rely on Him for everything. Papa God holds me close and gives me strategies. Jesus lovingly pours out the grace I need to do Papa's will. And the Holy Spirit teaches me and empowers me in ways that are Supernatural.

If we rely on God for every part of our walk, we will never come up wanting.

Reveal

We've recognized, responded, and put all our reliance on God. Now we're ready for the big reveal! What is it? Drumroll!

...I don't know.

Seriously. I mean, I know what it is for me, but I have no idea what it is for you. Don't fret. This is the fun part. You and God are hanging out, remember? When you hang out with someone a lot, you find that they have a lot to say. The same is true with God. The more you hang out with Him, the more you'll hear. Ask Him about His plans for you. And ask Him to reveal your assignment in this season.

We each have a destiny and a calling. **Our calling as believers doesn't change. We are called into fellowship with God's Son, Jesus Christ—this is the first and highest calling. From this position, we can love others as ourselves and carry out the great commission (Matthew 16:19-20). The way we carry out our calling, however, differs from**

person to person according to their individual design and changes from season to season according to God's assignment.

To be clear, our calling remains the same, our assignments do not. Like the Sons of Issachar, who understood the signs of the times, our assignment changes according to the time and seasons (1 Chron 12:32).

As I write this, our world is in crisis. There are so many critical situations happening all at once, it's making my head spin and my heart ache. Every day I hear of a new catastrophic situation. On one especially difficult day, I turned to Papa God in tears.

"I don't know what to do. There's so much that needs to be done, but I don't know how to do it. What do I do, God?"

He responded gently, with great tenderness. *"What did I ask you to do?"*

I knew what He asked me to do. I was already doing it, but it didn't seem to me to be enough. *"But what about all these other things?"*

Lovingly, patiently, *"I didn't design you for those. I have others that I've designed and assigned to be on the front lines of those areas. I designed you to do what I asked you to do. You're doing great. Just keep doing your part, and they'll do there's. And remember, the battle belongs to Me."*

I share this with you because there may come a time when you want to do more than what God has assigned you in a particular season, or you want to do something different. Maybe you'll think that what you're doing isn't enough. If God called you to the assignment then it is. He doesn't make mistakes. It's critical that you stick to the plan—His plan.

Spend time with God. Ask Him what He wants to reveal through you in this season and how He wants you to do it. Be willing to shift your assignment from what you did last season if He asks you to.

Before I move on from this subject, I feel like some of you are wondering if you're hearing Him correctly. You're not sure if you should move forward because you don't want to make a mistake. I've been there myself, so I totally get it. I encourage you to go with what is on your heart and then give God permission to redirect. Sometimes, He just wants us to step out in faith. He wants us to trust His ability to speak and our ability to hear. Perhaps He's teaching you to hear differently by giving you a knowing, or an inkling, instead of a megaphone or a neon sign. Go with it and trust Him to guide you. If your heart is to do the will of your Father, He's definitely not going to leave you hanging.

Represent

When you have your assignment, carry it out with care. Do it well, for you are representing, *re- presenting* God through everything you create. The Bible gives us many examples of how to do this. Here are a few:

- Be an ambassador for Christ. (2 Cor 5:20)
- Imitate Him (Eph 5:1)
- Proclaim the One who drew you out of darkness into light. (1 Peter 2:0)
- Walk in a manner worthy of Him. (Eph 4:1-3)
- Glorify God by bearing much fruit. (John 15:16)
- Shine your light in such a way that whatever you do points to God and gives Him glory. (Mat 5:14-16)
- Do everything in the name of Jesus, giving gratitude to God. (Col 3:17)

As creatives, we walk the tension between having the light shine on us and shining our light on Christ. If we paint a beautiful painting, write a great book, invent a terrific new tool, come up with a brilliant solution that increases company sales by 300%, etc, people will want to sing our praises. And therein lies the tension.

Years ago, after an especially powerful worship experience, I told the worship leader how great they were and how much I loved their set. He reacted with a great deal of discomfort. "Oh no, it's not me. It's all the Lord." I was new to the faith then and remember feeling embarrassed, like I said something wrong. Years later, I heard a speaker (I can't remember who it was) who had a similar encounter to mine.

He responded with, "Really? Because if it was all the Lord, I think it would have been much better." Ok, so that may not have been the nicest response, but you catch the drift.

When we are representing Jesus well, we are all in. We adhere to the scriptures referenced above, but we don't disappear from the equation. It's 100% Him and 100% us. While it may be uncomfortable to accept a compliment, we can accept it gracefully because it is the Lord who gives us grace. **We can create because He first created. We are able to do so because of what He did. We can be thankful for the gifts He has given us and acknowledge Him for them while at the same time accept our contribution. It's not about showing off but rather acknowledging our part in showing Him off.** How does it benefit God to hide our accomplishment when the very fact of our existence is meant to glorify Him? We glorify God when we live out His plan for our lives and collaborate with Him in our creative expression. God's glory is seen and experienced through us.

The problem comes when one tries to take all the credit. All creativity originates in the Master Creator. He is the only One who can make something out of nothing. By the same token, He designed and destined His offspring to reflect His creative nature. Therefore, we do Him a great disservice if we deny His ability to work through us. If I didn't paint a painting, no one could experience God through it. We take what begins in the heart and mind of God and bring it to bear.

Representing God well requires you to live a godly life, both publicly and privately, that honors Him. It requires an understanding that God is the source of all creativity, and He wants to express His heart through your work. And it requires ears to hear and eyes to see what God wants to say through you. It does not take a shrinking back but rather a thrust forward toward a greater expression of the fullness of God through the fullness of you.

I will add an extra "R" here for when you hit a wall or get derailed— REPEAT. Go back to the beginning and start this process all over again. Remind yourself about the magnitude of The Designer and your design. Recognize and respond. Rely on Him, not on yourself. Ask him to Reveal your next assignment and then carry it out and Represent Him well.

Talk with God

- Spend time in prayer:

  - Thank God for His creative nature that inspires awe and wonder.
  - Recognize that He designed you specifically and thank Him for creating you in His image and likeness to be creative.
  - Talk to Him about your desire to create with Him and for Him. Of course, He knows this, but He wants to hear it from your lips.
  - Talk and then listen. Write down what you hear, feel, or sense.

My Assignment

(original spoken word by Jill Wyckoff)

They say that the biggest failure is success in the wrong assignment.

I know I'm meant to go all the way to the top and drop like a bomb on the mountains and the meadows, testing the metal of my character against His.

Taking every thought, captive, actively pursuing appropriate passage to the glorious gates of His praise while at the same time resting in His presence all my days.

Breathe Him in, soak in the sweet fragrance of a love that can move mountains with a nod and form stars with a whisper; a love that is stronger than death, that loves me to the depth and breadth of unfathomable measure.

A love uncensored, unencumbered, unshakable, unequaled, not the essence of love, but love itself. HE IS LOVE itself!

He formed me to re form to retell His story over and over till that glorious day when He shall appear or I shall go home, and either way I am the blessed one.

Because I will never forget that once I was lost and now I am found and I am honor bound to spread His Word His truth, His light.

To lighten the path of the wayward.

Lighten the load of the burdened.

Light the way home to the Father who runs out to meet his son. His precious one.

The very one He delights in.

How can I know it and not show it? Now that would be a sin.

No, I am called. I am commissioned. And my mission is clear. As long as I'm here I will not hold back, not back down, not bow down to any other God but Jesus Christ.

The One, the Only, the King of Kings, and the Lord of Lords.

And as God is my witness I will witness of Him without fear.

I will confidently give a reason for the hope that I have.

I will run and not grow weary.

I will walk and not be faint.

I will soar on wings like eagles;

above the fray, beyond the expected, into the possible impossibilities that exist because of Him.

This is my assignment, my calling, my purpose; my very heart's desire.

He is my flame. I am on fire.

And I will not be quenched!

Section 2
Saying Yes

Chapter 6
Partnering With The Power

"And out of the ground the Lord God formed every animal of the field and every bird of the sky, and brought them to the man to see what he would call them; and whatever the man called a living creature, that was its name. The man gave names to all the livestock, and to the birds of the sky, and to every animal of the field, but for Adam there was not found a helper suitable for him."

— Genesis 2: 19-20 (NASB)

C AN YOU IMAGINE the Creator of everything asking you to partner with him in picking out the names of each living creature? It's not as though He couldn't think of names Himself. He is God, after all. But this very important, often overlooked scripture points to the fact that God desires to partner with us in creative pursuits.

I like to envision them sitting together, God and His pal Adam resting on a grassy knoll, shooting the breeze.

God, "Isn't it a beautiful day?"

Adam, "Absolutely perfect. Thank you for that, by the way."

"Don't mention it. Anything for you, my boy."

"Hey Pop, what do you call that thing over there?"

"Which thing, where?" (Pretending He doesn't know.)

"That brown creature eating that yellow thingy in the third tree from the right."

"Actually, I haven't thought about it. How about you give it a name? Better yet, why don't you name all of my creatures?"

"Really, Pop? What if I get it wrong?"

"Don't worry, you can't. I'm right here with you. You'll be great."

"I'll try."

"Adam, do or do not, there is no try."

"Ok, I'd like to call that one Monkey."

"Monkey, hmmm—I like the sound of that. Good job! One down and just a few thousand more to go!"

Alright, so I was cheeky and stole a line from Yoda, but you get the idea. Papa God must have been exceedingly proud to partner with his boy Adam. **The Bible says, *"whatever the man called each living creature, that was its name."* Not only does God reveal His desire to co-labor with man, but gives credence to the fact that man has an innate God-given ability to imagine. God did not doubt Adam's imagination, He encouraged him to exercise it.** With God by His side cheering him on, Adam knocked it out of the park.

My former pastor, Craig Muster, used to wonder if Adam named the creature and God transformed it in that instant to better fit its name. For example, a monkey didn't quite look like the monkey we know it to be until Adam named it. At that point, God finished their collaborative effort by reforming the monkey into its name. I like this picture. But regardless of whether or not this was actually the case, the partnership between God and man proved productive, perfect, and purposed.

God set a precedent in the garden of Eden. He shows us His heart to create with us, then and now. He hasn't changed His mind. He wants to partner with each and every one of us in everything we do and all we create. There are numerous examples in the Bible. Here's another one:

> *"Now the Lord spoke to Moses, saying, 'See, I have called by name Bezalel, the son of Uri, the son of Hur, of the tribe of Judah. And I have filled him with the Spirit of God in wisdom, in understanding, in knowledge, and in all kinds of craftsmanship, to create artistic designs for work in gold, in silver, and in bronze, and in the cutting of stones for settings, and in the carving of wood, so that he may work in all kinds of craftsmanship'"*
>
> — Exodus 31:1-5 (NASB)

Bezalel was the first person in the Bible to be *filled* with the Holy Spirit. Don't let this fact slip by you. Pause for a moment and consider the magnitude of this. As Christ-followers, we understand that God's Spirit indwells us. But this was before the resurrection of Jesus. Up until that time, the Holy Spirit may have fallen on or rested upon an individual, but this is the first mention of the Spirit of God indwelling someone—and that someone was not a soldier, a prominent leader, or a King—he was a craftsman.

God chose an artist—a creative—to partner with His Spirit to create His tabernacle. In doing so, He imbued him with wisdom, understanding, knowledge, and all kinds of creative skills. When we willingly partner with the Holy Spirit of God who lives in us, He teaches us everything we need to know and empowers us to do His will.

> *But the Advocate, the Holy Spirit, whom the Father will send in my name, will teach you all things and will remind you of everything I have said to you.*
>
> — John 14:26 (NIV)

Bezalel was taught to do the will of God by the greatest teacher of all, the Holy Spirit. But can you imagine how he must have felt at the beginning of his assignment? Sure, he was a creative guy and a decent leader, but out of all the men living at that time, God chose him. Some Bible translations say God *called him by name.*

"Bezalel...Bezalel."

"Uh, yes Lord. "

"Come create my dwelling place."

"Me?"

"Yes, you"

"But how, Lord? It is too big a task."

"I will help you. We will do it together."

No, this conversation is not in scripture; it is an echo of my own conversation with the Lord when He called me to create for Him. You see, He calls each one of us by name. He called Bezalel. He called me. And He's calling you. You have been chosen to create a dwelling place for Him.

> *"I consider it a privilege when He says to me, 'I want to use you and your artwork. I have need of you.' It is the Isaiah 6 experience. The Godhead calls out, 'Whom shall I send and who will go for us.' When I answer back as Isaiah did in his time, 'Yes, Lord, send me,' He then says, 'Go and paint to tell the people my heart.'"*
>
> — Jean Shen, Artist, San Diego CA

Bezalel means "overshadowed by God." What a stunning picture of perfect partnership. There is another one who was overshadowed by God. Her name was Mary, a young unmarried virgin who became the mother of our Savior. God called her to create a dwelling place for Him—quite literally.

> *"Then the angel said to her, 'Do not be afraid, Mary, for you have found favor with God. And behold, you will conceive in your womb and bring forth a Son, and shall*

*call His name Jesus. He will be great, and will be called
the Son of the Highest; and the Lord God will give Him
the throne of His father David. And He will reign over
the house of Jacob forever, and of His kingdom there will
be no end.'*

*Then Mary said to the angel, 'How can this be, since I do
not know a man?'*

*And the angel answered and said to her, 'The Holy Spirit
will come upon you, and the power of the Highest will
overshadow you; therefore, also, that Holy One who is
to be born will be called the Son of God. Now indeed,
Elizabeth your relative has also conceived a son in her
old age; and this is now the sixth month for her who was
called barren.*

For with God nothing will be impossible.'"

— Luke 1:30-37 (NKJV)

When God called Mary, the first thing He did was recognize that she just might be scared out of her mind. He assured her. "Do not be afraid. You are favored" (Luke 1:30 paraphrased). When you're face-to-face with the Angel of the Lord, I'm sure that's a very reassuring thing to hear. The next thing He does is explain her assignment. Note His choice of words; you *will* conceive; you *will* bring forth. These declarations leave no room for interpretation. Even still, the magnitude of what He's saying is a bit mind-blowing, and Mary responds out of her limitation, *"How can this be, since I do not know a man?"* This is where we all can relate to her. "How can this be," we say, "since I'm not good enough, talented enough...educated enough...qualified enough..." We all have reasons why we think God's calling couldn't possibly work. If you noticed, He did not sit and have a chat with her about her reasons. **God does not coddle mindsets rooted in fear or lack. Our current condition does not pose a threat to His plans. He was unfazed by Mary's situation, and He's not rattled by yours. Why?**

Because the power of the Holy Spirit—God Himself—will co-labor with us to manifest His decrees. His will *will* be done.

Mary was given the greatest assignment in history, to birth God in human form. She willingly accepted it even though it posed great risk and required an even greater sacrifice. She did so because she trusted God in the partnership. After all, He was the Father of the One she would birth.

Though our assignment is obviously not the same as Mary's, God is calling us to birth something, and it will involve a measure of risk and sacrifice. Be that as it may, we can rest assured that, just like Mary, God promises to co-labor with us. He is the Father of all creativity. Have faith in the Divine partnership. Trust that with Him, *nothing* is impossible. And like Adam, Bezalel, and Mary, say "Yes," and see what God will do through you.

Ponder in Your Heart:

- What can God do through His power in your current situation?
- Ponder the possibilities.
- Journal your thoughts.

Chapter 7
The Power Of Choice

"There is a tide in the affairs of men.
Which, taken at the flood, leads on to fortune;
Omitted, all the voyage of their life
Is bound in shallows and in miseries.
On such a full sea are we now afloat,
And we must take the current when it serves,
Or lose our ventures."

— William Shakespeare, Julius Caesar

MY FATHER HAD this Shakespeare quote hanging over his desk for as long as I can remember. He typed it on his old Remington typewriter, printed it, framed it, and moved it from house to house. In time, the paper yellowed and the print faded, but it continued to remind him to seize opportunities when they arise. Opportunities that pass by while you procrastinate may never present themselves again. In this quote from William Shakespeare's play, *Julius Caesar*, the character Brutus imagines life having an influence on both free will and destiny. Life's outcome, whether fortune or misery, is determined by our choices.

A few years ago, Darren Wilson spoke at one of our Kingdom

Creativity Conferences in San Diego. Darren wrote, directed, and produced a number of documentaries. In one of the conference sessions he shared the journey of his first film, *Finger of God (WP Films, 2007)*. In this film, Darren set out to see if God still works miracles and, if so, to capture them on film and make a case for their existence. *Finger of God* is brilliantly captivating and encouraging. Brae and I watched this documentary when we first discovered the power of the Holy Spirit, and it motivated us to press even harder into the greater things of God. I remember one story in particular that Darren shared at the conference. In the years after the film came out, he repeatedly heard, "Hey man, I loved *Finger of God*. It was awesome! I had that same idea to make a movie just like that." He heard this so many times that it became almost comical. But the point that he wanted to highlight was this, "When God asks you to do something, do it. If you don't, He may decide to give it to someone who will." Darren said he was not God's first, tenth, or even His sixteenth choice—he was simply the first one to say yes.

Darren said yes to making *Finger of God*. It wasn't easy. There were many challenges along the way, but God was faithful to see it completed through the one who was willing. It was the first film in a Divine partnership that would lead Darren Wilson to become founder and CEO of *Wanderlust Productions*, a film/television production company that focuses on creating media that advances the Kingdom of God worldwide.

There is so much that God can do through a willing partner. He wants to author your story and perfect your faith. There is only one way to test the level of your faith—walk it out. Trust that God will do what He says He will do.

> *"I pray with great faith for you, because I'm fully convinced that the One who began this glorious work in you will faithfully continue the process of maturing you and will put his finishing touches to it until the unveiling of our Lord Jesus Christ!"*
>
> — Philippians 1:6 (TPT)

When I said yes to God initially, it was not specifically in the realm of creative exploits. I told God that I wanted to live for Him, whatever that looked like. I said, "Papa, I'm all in." And I meant it. Until He asked me to paint in public. As you already know, I balked and backslid and buckled beneath the thought of doing anything in public. And you know what God did? He called me on it.

"Remember when you told me you were all in?"

"Yes, God."

"What is it about painting in public that makes it not part of the *all in* you were talking about?"

He had a good point. I had no clever comeback (and believe me, I have a lot of them). I couldn't rationalize or argue my way out of it. I had no excuse whatsoever. I simply had to say yes or renege on my promise to be *"all in,"* and the thought of that broke my heart. So as much as it pained me, emotionally and even physically, I had to say yes. I couldn't turn my back on God after all He had done for me. And, of course, that decision impacted my life in countless and wondrous ways. Even as I write this, I can feel the emotion rising. It makes me weep to think about all that God has done and is still doing in me and through me as a result of my yes.

In 2014, Brae and I went with Bill and Carol Dew of Dewnamis Ministries to minister with a church in Graz, Austria. It was a glorious experience that I will never forget. It was also my first time ministering through creativity in a country other than my own. On one of the days, the church scheduled a ministry outreach in a local park. We set up various stations for prayer and connection, and I chose a lovely patch of grass not too far from the prayer teams to set up my easel and paints. If you've ever been to Austria, you will probably agree that it is one of the most beautiful countries in the world. It's dreamlike. And so, on this particular day, I was motivated to paint the beauty I was experiencing. Surrounded by lush green lawns, multi-colored flowers in various shades of pinks and yellows, and the majestic Italian Alps standing guard in the distance, I began to paint. I didn't paint the grass or flowers or the mountain. I painted the essence of them—how they made me feel. This resulted in a spectacle of color and movement but no discernable features. People strolled up to watch. Some stayed long enough to see the painting take shape; some stayed only a few moments before going off to enjoy their day. There were a few people who seemed fascinated and struck up a conversation. And then there was Gertrude.

I had finished the painting and was removing my apron when I was approached by a very excited elderly woman. She grabbed my arm, and in a thick Austrian accent, she gushed, "How much is this painting? This painting is for me! I must have it!" I was quite surprised but also delighted. I explained that I was with a church but would ask the pastor if I could give it to her. "I don't think there will be a problem. I just need to go find her," I clarified. She was overjoyed and let me know that she would be back to check with me in a little while.

As you may have guessed, the pastor was pleased to give her the painting. It turned out that she knew the woman, Gertrude, and there was a much bigger story to unfold. The pastor explained to me that Gertrude's father was a Nazi who had done unthinkable acts against the Jews. Traumatized by this, Gertrude had suffered lifelong depression, anxiety, and a number of physical ailments as a result of the guilt and shame that she carried. Three years prior, Gertrude had been given a prophetic word for her healing. Apparently, I painted this word.

Let's park on this for a moment because it's too astounding to let it slip by without the attention it deserves—to God be the glory! I painted an abstract painting without any other thought than to gaze upon His beauty and paint what I felt the Holy Spirit was leading me to paint. The painting had no recognizable elements, no discerning forms. And yet, Gertrude saw the manifestation of her prophetic word; her healing within it. No wonder she was so excited; "This painting is for me! I must have it!" Only God, working Supernaturally through my creative expression, could have accomplished this.

Gertrude did get her painting and her healing. And if this isn't awe-inspiring enough, there's actually more to the story.

Gertrude had experienced severe emotional and physical effects resulting from the trauma of what her father, a Nazi, had done to the Jews. I am a Christian by my choice, but a Jew by my heritage.

Gertrude suffered greatly by what her father had done to the Jews, and God had a Jew paint her healing!

This testimony never fails to bring me to tears. It is a beautiful picture of Papa God's tender love, magnificent power, and absolute desire to impact lives through our creativity if we are willing to partner with Him. Had I not said yes to God, I would have robbed Gertrude of this blessing and robbed myself as well. We are blessed to be a blessing.

The Choice to Say Yes:

- What do you have to gain if you say yes?
- What do you have to lose if you ignore God's call or say no?
- Journal your thoughts.

I pray that you will rest assured in the One who designed you to create; the One who has a plan for you to create; the One who wants to co-labor with you to impact others through all you create. I pray you will put your hand in His and say YES.

You don't have to conquer the world today. It's okay to start out small. It's actually part of God's plan...

Chapter 8
Humble Beginnings

"Do not despise these small beginnings, for the Lord rejoices to see the work begin..."

— Zechariah 4:10 (NLT)

WE ALL HAVE to start somewhere. **Everything that came into being started with one simple step—a move toward a goal.** Even God started with one thing and then moved onto the next. His creation story, as outlined in Genesis, reveals a step-by-step process—heaven, earth, light, day, night, ocean, sky—one-by-one. It may not be our version of "humble beginnings," but it certainly outlines the perfect model for us to follow.

Now that you've said yes to God (or are considering it seriously), how do you begin your process?

Start with a baby step.

My baby step was painting at a worship event. I'm not gonna lie—it was terrifying. Baby steps take guts. But as they say, "No guts, no glory." Literally. When we move past our discomfort, we experience God's glory working in us and through us. I remember being scared to death at that event, and when it was over, I thought to myself with absolute astonishment, "It didn't kill me." Not only did it not kill me, it blessed me.

I had dreams of writing books, painting fabulous paintings; I let my imagination run wild. But if I had tried to start with my focus on the finish line, I never would have entered the race. I know myself well enough to know that I would have talked myself out of it. I would not have been ready. But when I started my journey with a baby step, half-hearted as it was, God met me in that place. When I started to fall, He caught me. When I doubted, He cheered me on. In the small beginnings, my faith increased. As God encountered me, my trust grew. This process moved me from one level to the next; glory to ever increasing glory. I grew in maturity so that I could accept bigger assignments and overcome greater obstacles. It wasn't always a pretty picture. There were times when I slid backwards. I took my eyes off the prize and cast them inward—spiraling down a BC (Before Christ) destructive path of *self*. Caught in a web of self-reliance, self-pity, self-consciousness, self-limitation, self-condemnation. I wondered if I could do anything right and why on earth God would want any part of me. These bouts may have lasted a day, a week, or a month, but looking back, I can see that they too were part of my process of maturing.

> *"The Lord makes firm the steps of the one who delights*
> *in him; though he may stumble, he will not fall, for the*
> *Lord upholds him with his hand."*
> — Psalm 37:23-24 (NIV)

These days, I still get sidetracked now and again, but not as frequently or as long in duration, which points to progress. Yay God! That is not to say I've arrived, though—far from it! None of us will ever *arrive*, which greatly reduces any pressure on our part to think that we have to.

> *" Not that I have already grasped it all or have already become perfect, but I press on if I may also take hold of that for which I was even taken hold of by Christ Jesus. Brothers and sisters, I do not regard myself as having taken hold of it yet; but one thing I do: forgetting what lies behind and reaching forward to what lies ahead, I press on toward the goal for the prize of the upward call of God in Christ Jesus."*
>
> — Philippians 3:12-14 (NASB)

That is what I do—I press on. I believe this is one of my best character traits. **Once I was shy and embarrassed about displaying any part of myself or my work. Now I am bold. It's not because of what I carry—It's because of WHO I carry.**

As I traveled the path of humble beginnings, I developed the "Just Do It" mentality. Nike® may have coined the phrase, but I stole it fair and square (at least to my way of thinking). I became the "Just Do it Girl." If I was afraid to do something, I'd do it anyway. I'd do it afraid. And because it didn't kill me and I ended up feeling blessed, I continued to do things I was afraid to do. Eventually, I wasn't afraid anymore, and I encouraged others to "Just do it." I watched them take their baby step, grow in boldness, experience the blessing, and this became my bliss. Even more than achieving anything on my own was the blessing I felt from being able to encourage others.

Process isn't always easy to walk through, but it is the only way to get from one place to another. I sincerely appreciate every step of my journey from where I started (scared to death and sick to my stomach) to where I am now. And I vow to appreciate the journey from where I am now to where I am going. **In the midst of the process is where we find out what we're made of; mine the gold within us and uncover the treasure that was always there beneath the surface waiting to be discovered. It's where God shows up in ways that you never dreamed possible and invites you to experience Him on a whole new level. It is an exhilarating adventure that begins with a single step and climbs to heights beyond your imagination.**

It is the adventure of a lifetime—yours.
Would you like to go?

Baby Steps:

1. Talk with God and ask Him to show you a way in which you can take one baby step forward.
2. Write down that first step.
3. Pray about it.
4. Do it (even if you have to do it afraid).
5. Journal your experience.
6. Repeat, starting with step 1.

Chapter 9
The Rhythm Of The Spirit

EVERY BABY STEP leads you somewhere. Only God knows exactly where, but we know He's got a plan and is up to something good because you're here. Whether you're starting a whole new creative journey, resurrecting an old one, or moving from one project to another, every starting place begins with a blank slate and an invitation.

For me, a blank slate looks like a blank document and a blank canvas. For my business, it starts with a worldwide web search or a conversation with a stakeholder. You will discover your own starting place, and when you do, you will have the opportunity to invite the Holy Spirit into your process. This is by far the most important step that any Kingdom-minded creative can take when starting anything. Please don't let this slip by without cementing it within your spirit.

Now to be clear, we recognize that He's already in us, willing and able to collaborate. But our pathway to God-sized success begins when we turn towards Him and extend a heartfelt invitation to the One who equips us for the Supernatural—the One who IS Supernatural.

My invitation looks something like this:

"God, I don't want to do this without You. Holy Spirit, thank You for guiding me and teaching me what I need to know. I invite You to partner with me, collaborate with me. Help me to move out of my own way. Help me to have eyes to see and ears to hear what You want to say and do. Help

me to do Your will so that Your glory may be experienced through my work. In Jesus name, amen."

Sometimes I just say, *"God help me!"* and He does. He's wonderfully gracious like that.

When you and the Holy Spirit are rolling forward in your process, there is a rhythm that takes place. It's listening and doing, waiting and responding. It can be a slow-paced Minuet that moves with graceful steps to a gently sweeping cadence. Or it can be a rigorous Latin Samba that maneuvers with precision to a heart-pounding beat. Regardless of the rhythm, our part is to move in step with God and let Him lead; to listen to His voice, and move to whatever beat He chooses without falling behind or jumping ahead. This Divine dance leads us to create Supernaturally.

I remember the first time I discovered this *pas de deux* with the Holy Spirit. It was early on in my creative journey while painting at an especially kinetic worship event. My husband helped me set up my station in the corner of this fairly small venue packed with people singing and dancing to the beat of numerous percussion instruments. It was all out halal worship, and it was powerful. But it was also rather loud. After he finished setting up, Brae went off to get me some coffee (He knows me so well). At this point, I invited the Holy Spirit to paint with me, and I felt a strong impression to paint blue. So I dragged my fingers through the blue paint and brushed them gently across the canvas. I was aware that the graceful motion of my hands seemed out of place juxtaposed against the loud drumming in the room, but the movement seemed right. I continued this delicate dance with the Holy Spirit, and in short order, Brae returned and handed me my coffee. Uncharacteristically, he grabbed a chair and brought it in to sit very closely to me. He stayed there right by my side for the remainder of the evening.

On the way home, Brae told me that he felt overwhelmed by the number of people packed into such a small space; between that and the dancing, drumming, and loud music, he felt unsettled. He said he was grateful to be able to leave to get the coffee. He planned to drop it off and spend the rest of the night in the car, but something happened when he handed me the cup. As he came close, he felt a profound sense of peace. "That's why I pulled the chair up to sit next to you," he said, "When I sat in your bubble, I felt completely peaceful."

I'm not sure if the Holy Spirit brought me there to paint that night just for this revelation and the ministry to my husband, but it's certainly possible. Unbeknownst to Brae, I was, in fact, painting an abstract expression of peace. I did not have any idea of what I would paint that night as I stood in front of my blank canvas. But once the Spirit prompted me to paint with varying hues of blue in particularly graceful movements, I knew we were dancing a slow dance. In this gentle sway, I felt the manifestation of His peace take hold and pour onto the canvas. What I did not know is that it radiated out from the canvas into the atmosphere around me.

From that point on, I knew that anytime I painted with the Spirit of God I had the ability (by His ability) to shift the atmosphere. It didn't matter if I painted at a brewery or a beach; a secular venue or a church. I moved in the authority of one who carries the power and presence of the Holy Spirit of God within me. He's proved over and over again that He can do more than I can ask or imagine according to His power that is at work within me. (Ephesians 3:20). Before that evening with Brae in my bubble, I never imagined I could shift the atmosphere through painting.

And then there is the flow.

As we dance to the rhythm of our Lord, we will begin to get into the flow. The steps become easier. Our movement becomes less robotic. We think to ourselves, "I got this," and maybe we do. But maybe we don't. And therein lies the challenge of being in the flow.

This week, they brought back *Star Wars: Empire Strikes Back* (*20th Century Fox, 1980*) in the theaters for its 40th anniversary. My husband is the biggest *Star Wars* fan I've ever known, so of course, we purchased tickets and celebrated ESB's 40th (and our first time back in the theater since the Covid pandemic). Watching again on the big screen, I saw so many things I hadn't seen before or plain old forgot (I tend to do that from time to time). In one scene, Luke is training with Yoda and feels the urge to rush off and rescue his friends Han and Leia. Master Jedi,

Yoda, tells Luke he's not ready to do this on his own. They even bring an ethereal opaque looking Obi-Wan Kenobi back from the grave to convince Luke not to go. Does he listen? Nope. Like a cocky, entitled, rookie Jedi, he argues that he's had enough training—he doesn't need anyone else—he's good to go. Soon afterwards, we see him face-to-face with the evil Darth Vader, and he's not so cocky now. He realizes that he's no match for his nemesis and pleads, "Obi-Wan help me!"

Maybe this isn't the best example, but I can see all of us in young Luke. We've had some training and experience; we've had some successes under our belt, and now we think we're ready for the big leagues. We've got the calling and the assignment. Surely we can do this on our own. As we see by this example of Luke in *Empire Strikes Back,* this attitude almost led to his destruction—and it can lead to ours as well.

We cannot create without "The Force" and expect to win against our evil nemesis. With God, all things are possible, and without Him, nothing is possible. Victory is in the Lord. Invite Him in for the win!

Getting Real:

- Invite the Holy Spirit to dance with you the next time you create.
- Note any shift in the atmosphere that you're aware of.
- What is something that you think you've got down pat?
- Invite God into it and see what He says or does.

Chapter 10
The Creative Lifestyle

W<small>E HAVE BEEN</small> called to create for the purpose of extending the Kingdom. Whether it's in the ministry or the marketplace, whether we create for free or earn our living from it, creativity is how we serve the Lord and bless others. But how do we consistently stay in the flow of the Holy Spirit and progress in our calling? We cultivate a lifestyle of connection.

Your creative expression is directly affected, positively or negatively, by the level of connection you have with your Creator.

Let it stand for the record, I am no saint. I have my ups and downs—certainly more downs than I'd like. Maybe you can relate. As I mentioned previously, if I let my eyes wander away from Jesus for any length of time, I find myself back-sliding down a slippery slope of *self.* These are the days when I feel like I'm drowning in a sea of emotion, overly sensitive to every little thing, irrationally irrational, and fighting (needlessly) for my next breath. In this state, I find it difficult to hear God's tender voice over my own shrewish one. I can express myself creatively and produce good things but not God things. Of course, this isn't too surprising since He isn't invited to my pity party.

If you're at all like me, I want you to take courage. Though being ruled by your emotions isn't Godly or productive, your sensitivity is not a curse but a blessing. It's God's heart connected to yours; the birthplace of creativity.

The fact is, we creatives are highly sensitive, deeply feeling people by nature. God designed us this way—to be sensitive to others, to our surroundings, to the highs and lows of the life we lead and the world we live in. We are compassionate and caring. We love justice and righteousness. We are attracted to beauty and repelled by evil. We have been fashioned for a standard of sensitivity that allows God to collaborate with us in our creative expression to influence culture rightly and encounter people on a primal level.

God-centered sensitivity looks like Jesus. **God, in human form, was surrounded by suffering and injustice. He felt every possible emotion. And yet, He was so connected to His Father that He did not buckle nor bow to lesser worldly gods: angst, fear, shame, rejection, hopelessness, or pride. In vulnerability and humility, with all His emotions in tow, Jesus reassured and sustained Himself through intentional connection with the source of absolute truth and perfect love—His Daddy.**

God-centered sensitivity is objective—based on the fact that we are created to love and be loved by the One who *is* Love. Jesus is the standard. Creativity birthed out of our God-given sensitive nature in line with His will and in collaboration with His Spirit is Supernatural.

On the opposite side of the spectrum is human-centered sensitivity. Humanism sets the standard according to the individual's thoughts and ideals, which are rooted in their emotions, personal experiences, societal influences, and other fluctuating factors. It is subjective. Google dictionary defines humanism as "an outlook or system of thought attaching prime importance to human rather than divine or Supernatural matters." Individuals operating from humanistic sensitivity may be guided by a genuine will to do good, but their standard of good leaves God out of the equation. The humanist word on the street says, "You do your truth, and I'll do mine." This may get a round of high fives for being politically correct but the problem arises when one's individual truth (their standard of right and wrong) infringes on the life of another. I'm not saying that those who create from this place cannot produce something positive and beneficial, but it falls short of God's standard. We see this over and over again throughout our society in our movies, music, tv shows, and literature. The humanist standard bows to an ever-changing popular opinion, which in turn influences a culture of confusion and propagates a worldly agenda that most often opposes the nature and will of God.

You and I are called to God's standard of sensitivity. As Christian creatives, we have been chosen to present Godly works, ideas, innovations, and systems unshackled by unrighteousness and harmful agendas. But how do we do this when we live in a world where humanism influences every area of our society? We are assaulted on all sides with images, ideals, and systems that promote man's opinion, not God's truth. How do we keep from drowning in a sea of emotion that contaminates our creativity?

Our sensitive nature is a gift from God. Therefore, we must connect with the Giver.

> *"Let us fix our eyes on Jesus, the author and perfecter of our faith, who for the joy set before him endured the cross, scorning its shame, and sat down at the right hand of the throne of God. Consider him who endured such opposition from sinful men, so that you will not grow weary and lose heart."*
>
> — Hebrews 12:2-3 (NIV)

Fixing our eyes on Jesus is not just a good idea, it is the life force that drives our creativity and keeps us on solid ground.

The key: Connect and disconnect.

I have learned that I cannot watch certain TV shows or movies because they influence my thoughts, dreams, and emotions. At the beginning of my creative journey, I discovered that there were certain shows that left me feeling agitated and moody afterwards. I never really noticed it before. The same happened when watching news or spending a lot of time on social media. I'd feel depressed and miserable afterwards.

I realized it was a wake-up call from God to keep my thoughts from being contaminated, so I stopped watching shows that were offensive to my God-given sensibilities. I also eliminated or limited my time in any area that influenced me negatively. This included social media, music, movies, YouTube videos, memes, books, magazines. It also included gossip.

"Above all else, guard your heart, for everything you do flows from it. Keep your mouth free of perversity; keep corrupt talk far from your lips. Let your eyes look straight ahead; fix your gaze directly before you. Give careful thought to the paths for your feet and be steadfast in all your ways. Do not turn to the right or the left; keep your foot from evil." - Proverbs 4:23-27 (NIV)

Our creativity flows from our heart. Our hearts are influenced by what we take in, what we see and hear. If we are intentional to stand guard over our hearts, feed ourselves on the will of God; think on that which is true, noble, right, pure, lovely, admirable, excellent, and praiseworthy, we will produce good fruit.

I'm not saying it's easy, or that everyone is called to the same level of censorship that I am. There are days I click through Netflix, Amazon Prime, Hulu, and Disney like a madwoman trying to find something... anything...to watch. Good God, is there anything decent to watch that isn't rated TV-MA?! Even the TV-13's and -14's are iffy nowadays (at least for me). I think I've watched every Hallmark movie out there, certainly the Christmas films, and every one of Monk's 125 episodes. I've managed to find a few other benign television series, but the pickings are getting slimmer and my irritation is growing fatter. If only there were more quality programs to choose from!

And there could be. If we created them.

Folks, we are the solution—the solution to this and to so much more.

God is calling us to walk in dominion and authority; to display the glory of God to the world. We have been designed to create works of brilliant imagination executed with excellence; works that promote His values. This takes consistent and intentional connection with Him, the source of sanctified creativity. It involves a lifestyle of sacrifice and worship. Our life bears witness to Jesus.

> *"Therefore I urge you, brothers and sisters, by the*
> *mercies of God, to present your bodies as a living and*
> *holy sacrifice, acceptable to God, which is your spiritual*
> *service of worship. And do not be conformed to this*
> *world, but be transformed by the renewing of your mind,*
> *so that you may prove what the will of God is, that which*
> *is good and acceptable and perfect."*
> — Romans 12: 1-2 (NASB)

How do we become a living sacrifice, worshipping God with our whole lives? How do we stay in the flow of the Holy Spirit?

We live the life God intended for us to live. We walk in ever-increasing fullness of His design for our lives. We say yes to His calling and step into our assignment to create with and for Him. And if we happen to sidetrack or backtrack, we don't berate, belittle, or give up; we reconnect.

How do we connect?

We develop spiritual disciplines that can be exercised and strengthened like muscles.

The first thing that comes to mind is to see what God Himself has to say to us. St. Jerome said, "The Scriptures are shallow enough for a babe to come and drink without fear of drowning and deep enough for a theologian to swim in without ever touching the bottom." Whether you're a new believer or a long-time Christian, there is much to be gained by cracking open a Bible and diving in. God's Word reveals His nature, His wisdom, and His heart for you. I find that when I spend time each day, even if it's just a few minutes on especially hectic days, I always feel refreshed, strengthened, and loved. I especially enjoy all the many Bible versions that are available now. Growing up, I had only King James, which is beautiful but was hard for me to comprehend. I later discovered modern versions with language I could understand,

and this opened up a whole new world to me. When I read His Word, God breathes life into my tired soul and makes me aware of how near and present He is in all my circumstances. If I miss a day of reading my Bible, I don't berate myself, but I definitely feel the difference.

> *"This Book of the Law shall not depart from your mouth, but you shall meditate on it day and night, so that you may be careful to do according to all that is written in it; for then you will make your way prosperous, and then you will achieve success."*
>
> — Joshua 1:8 (NASB)

Another way to connect with Papa is through worship. At our old church, The Awakening, we used to say, "Worship is the key to everything." When we turn our affection towards God, our hearts align with His. We see only Him; everything else falls away. We experience the reality that He is bigger than anything we face; that He is our ever-present help in times of trouble; that He loves us beyond anything in our human experience. We inhale His perfect love and exhale new life. Worship is the overflow of the adoration we have for Papa God; our response to the One who created us and gave His son to save us.

I love to sing and dance. I cannot keep quiet or remain still when I hear music. Regardless of how well I do either of those things, it makes no difference. These creative expressions are in me—they're a part of my design. I believe all children are born with a love for singing and dancing. I have witnessed countless babies shaking their booty to the beat. Oftentimes, before they can even walk. Singing seems to come naturally as well. I have a cherished video of my 3-year-old granddaughter, Juliet, singing at the top of her lungs at last year's church Christmas pageant. Miss Nancy encouraged all the kids to project, and my darling Jules let her little light shine so bright that the parents couldn't help but burst out laughing. This is a beautiful example of pure, unpretentious, unabashed worship to the Lord. It's exactly what King David did. It didn't matter if he was undignified or that his wife was embarrassed by him. The only thing that mattered was his worship. He wrote in Psalm 34, "*I will bless the Lord at all times; His praise shall continually be in my mouth. My soul will make its boast in the Lord. The humble will hear it and rejoice. O magnify the Lord with me, and let us exalt His name together.*" (NASB).

There are many ways to worship our Lord. Besides singing and dancing to worship music, I also like to write poetry and journal. Sometimes I sit quietly amongst nature and thank Him for the majesty of His beautiful creation. I listen intently for His gentle whisper through the breeze—close my eyes and breathe Him in through the scent of the woodland trees. My friend, Tracy, loves to worship God as she rides her bike throughout the winding hills of La Jolla—taking in the beauty of His creation with the wind whipping through her hair and the sun warming her skin. It's her special time with her Papa God, and they have wonderful conversations together as she pedals through town.

Our worship is otherworldly intimate. And just as our creativity is expressed in countless ways, so too is our worship. Find the ways that suit you, and then worship Him in Spirit and truth. In this deep connection to the One who is worthy of all our affection, honor, and adoration, your soul will find its home.

> "*The fire on the altar must be kept burning; it must not go out. Every morning the priest is to add firewood and arrange the burnt offering on the fire.*"
> — Leviticus 6: 12-13 (NIV)

From this place of connection to God through His Word and your worship, it is natural to move right into prayer—an intimate conversation between you and your Creator—your spirit and His. We talk, and He listens. He talks, and we listen. It's a Divine heart-to-heart exchange that connects us to the will of our Father.

When we disconnect from worldly perspectives and connect to Papa God, our creative expressions will reflect His righteousness. As

a result of Divine connection and collaboration, our natural abilities will take on Supernatural power. This is the life of a creative devoted to the One who calls them to create—a life lived in the flow of the Holy Spirit.

Produce Good Fruit:

- What are some things you can do to stand guard over your heart and mind?
- What are the ways you will personally connect with God?
- What things will you consider disconnecting from in order to maintain a creative lifestyle?
- Research Spiritual Disciplines and incorporate them into your lifestyle.

"...I urge you to live a life worthy of the calling you have received."

— Ephesians 4:1 (NIV)

Chapter 11
Obstacles To Obedience

"For our struggle is not against flesh and blood, but against the rulers, against the powers, against the world forces of this darkness, against the spiritual forces of wickedness in the heavenly places."

— Ephesians 6:12 (NASB)

RESISTANCE. COMPARISON. PERFECTION. Performance. Rejection. Shame. Guilt. Disqualification. Devaluation. Discouragement. Procrastination. Distraction. Malaise. Writer's block or brain block. Sound familiar? Every creative will deal with any or all of these at some point or another. Why? Because there is an enemy of our soul who wages war on creativity. His name is Satan; he is the Father of Lies.

Oh, and he has a vicious, jealous streak.

First, he was jealous of God. In Isaiah 14:12-15 we see that he wanted to be like the Most High. It wasn't enough for him to have beauty, power, and position. He wanted it all—he wanted to be worshipped as God. As a result, Satan was cast out of heaven along with a third of the angels who fell with him. He and his network of demon powers have been given a period of time to rule here. Their mission: steal, kill, and destroy (John 10:10).

Satan was jealous of God, and now he's jealous of you. Why? Because you can do something that he can't. You, my friend, can create.

Creativity originates in the heart and mind of God. As His offspring, made in His image and likeness, human beings have the ability to create. Satan was not created in the image and likeness of God, therefore, he does not have this ability. This drives him mad.

Let's take it one step further. As Christians, we have the Holy Spirit living in us, which allows us to create together with God—not just any creative works, but Supernatural expressions that glorify our Father. This is like pouring vinegar in the gaping wound of Satan's pus-filled ego!

As you can imagine, our enemy is mad as hell, and he's fighting back the only way he knows how. He can't create, but he can twist, tweak, and distort. One lie here, another lie there, and before you know it, he's got you thinking that you're a worthless, no-talent who doesn't have the right to be creative in any way whatsoever. The Father of Lies can be very convincing.

I started writing this book because God impressed upon me to do so. It was His idea, not mine. And I responded to Him with a sense of excitement. I told my husband, a writer of multiple books, that I was going to write on Supernatural creativity. He thought it was a wonderful idea and encouraged me greatly. The Father of Lies (FOL), however, did not think it was such a wonderful idea.

FOL: "Really?" (subtle insertion of doubt)

Me: "I think so." (already starting to second guess myself)

FOL: "Nobody knows who you are. You're not famous or anything. Who do you think you are, Theresa Dedmon?" (enter comparison and mockery)

Me: "Well, I know I'm not Theresa. But maybe somehow people will find my book. If it helps even one person, that will be worth it." (defense mechanism in response to feeling shame)

FOL: "Yeah, maybe one person will read it. Hell, maybe even a few people will read it. But is it really worth going to all that trouble? And what about your finances? Do you want to throw away all that money to produce a book that hardly anyone will read and maybe no one will like?" (add lack mindset, rejection, devaluation)

Me: "You got a point." (agreeing)

FOL: "And don't forget about all the other famous Christian artists besides Theresa that are killing it with their books. They've made a name for themselves. They have agents and publishers. They're real authors, not wannabes." (working to seal the deal with doubt, comparison, lack, rejection, devaluation, performance)

Me: "Ok, let me think about it some more." (replaying his words over and over; feeling ashamed, stupid, and pretty much worthless as a writer)

This is the point where I have the choice to bow out or move forward; disqualify myself and disconnect from my assignment, or take every thought captive and roll forward.

> "We are destroying arguments and all arrogance raised against the knowledge of God, and we are taking every thought captive to the obedience of Christ,"
>
> — 2 Cor 10:5 (NASB)

The reality is that I will have to take thoughts captive over and over again, daily, sometimes hourly, and at times even every few minutes until I've got my breakthrough. This is par for the course for every creative. Even in saying this, you can see how clearly it points to the lack of creativity and ingenuity in the mind of the enemy. Satan's system for success is regurgitation and intimidation. It's simple but effective, so I guess he's thinking if it ain't broke, don't fix it.

The flaw in Satan's plan to silence God's army of creatives is that he's already shown his hand. We know how he operates: sell subtle believable lies. It's true that there are times when his lies are so subversive that we don't see them coming. He even engages unsuspecting people around us, friends and family, to substantiate these false beliefs. It's pretty convincing. But his voice gives him away every time. It sounds like hopelessness. When you hold his words up to the light of The Word, it's so easy to see the difference. To put it bluntly, the enemy makes you feel like crap, and Jesus makes you feel perfectly loved. There's no mistaking the two.

There are a number of weapons in the enemy's arsenal, but here are a few you may recognize:

Comparison:

Who are you to do anything? Have you seen so-and-so's work? Do you think you're anywhere close to their level? Are you kidding me? It's kind of embarrassing. You don't have that kind of talent. You're too old. You're too young. You're not educated—not classically trained. The list goes on and on but you get the picture. We've all had these lines rolling around in our head—it's the voice of the Mocker—the enemy of our souls.

I spent most of my life comparing myself to others and coming up short. This drastically shaped every decision I made, which in turn led me down some really dark roads. I treated myself according to the little value I felt I was worth. This transcended all areas of my life, including creativity.

Comparison leads to disqualification by paralysis. It turns a blind eye to the fact that we were created uniquely to reveal God's heart in a way that only we can do. It denies diversity and God's plan to extend his kingdom through each and every one of his children. It believes that God did not create you with everything you need to fulfill His plans through you. It believes in a lesser god.

I cannot tell you how many times I have witnessed individuals with incredible creative gifts fall prey to the demonic power of comparison. I am shocked when I encounter artists who are embarrassed to show me their work because they think it's not good enough only to discover that it's exceptional. It never ceases to amaze me how these artists have been silenced by comparison, and yet they have so much to offer. Everyone can see it. Everyone except them, that is.

On the flip side, I've seen creatives of ALL levels across numerous disciplines create with God to release works and innovative ideas that encounter people Supernaturally. Recently, I've been doing a lot of doodles. It's not something I ever really practiced before; it's just what God is doing in this season through me. I don't think of doodles when I think of masterful works, but I know if The Master is sparking me to do them, there's a reason for it. One night while doodling, I asked Him if it was possible to prophesy through a doodle. The very next morning, I had an encounter with a couple of gals who talked about God leading them both in unusual ways. They used words of color and movement to describe this. Interesting, I thought, and then showed them the doodle I had been working on the night before. "Yes, it's exactly like that!" they both exclaimed. I had my answer. Thank you, Lord. I have since witnessed God touch people's lives on a number of occasions through my doodles. If I had compared them to my friend's museum-quality art, I would have discounted my own value and, in doing so, discounted the value of God's work through me. Isn't that just what the enemy would have us do?

There is only one person we should ever compare ourselves to. That's Jesus. Though we will never measure up on all accounts, we are to become more and more Christlike. In becoming more like Jesus we do not lose ourselves but rather become a greater version of ourselves—a fuller expression of our original design.

Jealousy:

Jealousy goes hand-in-hand with the spirit of comparison. It is its ugly offspring. Jealousy is rooted in a worldly limitation that pits one person against another. It says you can do something I can't, and that makes me feel bad. Jealousy can eat you alive with parasitic precision infesting you with an insufferable victim mentality. If the enemy can keep us focused on our own pitiful state of lack (victim mindset), then we will remain motionless and feel animosity towards those who do not. That's a win-win in the enemy's playbook.

God's Word says in James 3:14-16 (TPT), "*But if you harbor bitter envy and selfish ambition in your hearts, do not boast about it or deny the truth. Such 'wisdom' does not come down from heaven but is earthly, unspiritual, demonic. For where you have envy and selfish ambition, there you find disorder and every evil practice."* Sounds like the devil's playground to me.

In the Kingdom, when our brother or sister succeeds in their God-given assignment, we celebrate their victory. There is no competition—no jealousy. We understand that our mission is the same: to glorify God through our creative expression and see Jesus get His reward. In this, a win for one is a win for the Kingdom, and a win for the Kingdom is a win for all.

Perfectionism:

Who is perfect? Jesus. That's it. The rest of us have no shot at perfection. This isn't derogatory. It's a good thing. It should remove any attempt to try.

The Father of Lies works to keep us running on a hamster wheel of futility, chasing after perfectionism as a righteous goal and a noble prize. Meanwhile, he's offside snickering at the knowledge that this race will never be won. And worse, that some of us will die trying.

Successful American artist, author, and filmmaker, Julia Cameron hits the nail on the head in *The Artist's Way* (Tarcher/Perigee 1992), where she said, "Perfectionism is a refusal to let yourself move ahead. It is a loop—an obsessive, debilitating closed system that causes you to get stuck in the details of what you are writing or painting or making and lose sight of the whole. 'A painting is never finished. It simply stops in interesting places,' said Paul Gardner. A book is never finished. But at a certain point, you stop writing it and go on to the next thing. A film is never cut perfectly, but at a certain point, you let go and call it done. That is a normal part of creativity—letting go. We always do the best that we can by the light we have to see by."

Performance:

Performance is the pathway to perfectionism. Many of us were raised to experience love based on how well we performed. Be a good girl and you'll get a treat. Do all the right things and you will be appreciated. Maybe if you're good enough, smart enough, talented enough, we'll notice you. **Performance says you must continuously strive to be better than you are. Not from a healthy sense of personal growth and maturity, but because the familiar whip of failure might strike at any moment. Performance bears the scars of not being enough.**

Jesus knows a thing or two about scars. He paid the price for all our wrong-doings and inadequacies. The Bible says in Romans 3:23, *"for all have sinned and fall short of the glory of God." All* of us. And yet, our gracious Papa God didn't wait to love us until we performed perfectly. No. He demonstrated so much love for us that while we were in the midst of our sin He sent His perfect Son to take our place on the cross. In Christ, we are enough because He is enough. You cannot do anything to make God love you any more. And you cannot do anything to make God love you any less. **Our destiny is not based on our performance—it is based on our surrender.**

Rejection:

The internet affords us a wonderful opportunity to reach a worldwide audience. Many Christians are using the web to promote a message of hope and righteousness. It is truly an incredible gift to be able to connect with people all over the earth and see God's impact on their lives. However, as much as the internet provides a vehicle for good, it is also a skillful tool in the hand of the enemy.

Sadly, social media data reveals a devastating increase in suicides, especially in young children and teens who do not have the coping skills and/or the support to handle the inevitable rejection. In addition to an increase in suicides, there is a rapid rise in clinical depression as humanity surfs social platforms for significance and gets slammed by wave after wave of rejection. While there are many of us who have escaped those life-threatening swells, I think that most of us will admit to struggling against the tide. Check these off if you can relate:

- I check my posts throughout the day to see if I have received comments or likes.
- I'm disappointed and feel bad when there are no responses.
- When someone disagrees with my opinion, I second guess what I wrote.
- When my friends get more responses to their posts, it feels like they're accepted and I'm not.
- Sometimes I wonder why I post at all. Who cares?

All of us can probably relate to some, if not all, of these. The Internet is just one area where we experience the repeated sting of rejection. There is also our family, our work, our church, our friendships, and even our marriages. Anywhere we interact with people there is the possibility of rejection. But remember, people are not our enemy. Our fight isn't with flesh and blood but with spiritual forces of evil (Eph 6:12). Rejection is the language of lies spoken by the Father of Lies and his demonic minions.

In Christ, we lack nothing—no good thing (Psalm 23:1). We never have to fear rejection because we are accepted in the Beloved. We are the sons and daughters of the One true God, the Master Creator who created us to create. Our confidence and competence are in Him.

> *"Such is the confidence we have toward God through Christ. Not that we are adequate in ourselves so as to consider anything as having come from ourselves, but our adequacy is from God,"*
>
> — 2 Corinthians 3:4-5 (NASB)

Because our confidence is in Christ and our competence comes from God, we can rest assured that man's rejection has no bearing on us. The Bible addresses this in Galatians 1:10, "*Am I now trying to win*

*the approval of human beings, or of God? Or am I trying to please people?
If I were still trying to please people, I would not be a servant of Christ."*

As servants of Christ, we create for Him and with Him. Our partner is God Himself. With Him we cannot fail.

Fear:

Fear is the main ingredient in every weapon formed by the enemy—which by the way, are weapons that cannot prosper (Isaiah 54:17). Comparison, jealousy, perfectionism, performance, rejection, pride, anxiety, and every other tool of the enemy's trade is grounded in fear. Fear is a sticky spidery web that wraps around our heart and tries to squeeze the life out of us. **Fear causes us to take short breaths and live small lives. It tells us that it's okay to stay in our comfort zone. It pitches in and helps us build a safety net around ourselves. Fear whispers, "Just give up. Take the easy way out. It won't cost you anything." In reality, it will cost you everything. It will cost you your God-given destiny.** It will rob you of your blessings and rob others of the blessings that God planned to bring through you.

I heard Bill Johnson, pastor of Bethel Church in Redding CA, speak on this subject. He said, "I cannot afford to have a thought that didn't originate in the heart of God." This means that we have to break our alliance with the enemy and break off any agreements we've made about ourselves and our destiny that are not Kingdom-oriented. As we step out and go for our dreams, we find out what we really believe. Are we "fully persuaded that what God has promised He is able to perform?" (Romans 4:21)

Fear or faith?

Imagine your heavenly Father approaching. He sees you, and breaks out into a huge grin. His pace quickens with excitement; He's practically running towards you. He's close enough now that you can see His eyes sparkling as they lock in with yours. He reaches His hand out towards you.

Take it.

Your hand is now in the hand of perfect love. Perfect love is the answer.

> *"There is no fear in love, but perfect love drives out fear, because fear involves punishment, and the one who fears is not perfected in love."*
> — 1 John 4:18 (NASB)

When we are in the presence of Papa's perfect love, fear is replaced with a certainty that the Lord is on our side and with Him, all things are possible. We are never alone. He will never leave us or forsake us. His love is not conditional; it will not be retracted. We are convinced of our safety in Him.

> *"For I am convinced that neither death, nor life, nor angels, nor principalities, nor things present, nor things to come, nor powers, nor height, nor depth, nor any other created thing will be able to separate us from the love of God that is in Christ Jesus our Lord."*
> — Romans 8:38-39 (NASB)

I've now written in the neighborhood of 3,000 words in this chapter about the enemy and the creative. I suppose I could easily write another 3,000, but honestly, I don't want to give him that much time or credit. The bottom line is that he loathes Kingdom-minded creatives, and he's doing his best to silence us. Yes, he's noisy and annoying, but that's because he knows his time is limited. He's fully aware that God has already won the battle over him. Let us also be fully aware of the win and step into our victorious creative calling.

Response Time:

- Next time you're tempted to play movies over and over in your head, ask yourself if you are magnifying your heavenly Father or the Father of Lies? If you're not imagining God's plan for your life and replaying those movies, then take a moment to repent and pivot. (No condemnation—another one of Satan's tools)

- Ask God to highlight areas where you have been swayed by the lies of the enemy. Write them down and bring them to the light. Submit them to God and the next time you're tempted to believe those lies, resist. The Bible says resist the devil and he will flee. (James 4:7) Choose to resist.

- Put your faith into action. Ceate. That's the worst thing you can do to the enemy. Vincent van Gogh said, "*If you hear a voice within you say you cannot paint, then by all means paint and that voice will be silenced.*" Paint, write, sing, dance, think, imagine, dream, then do. CREATE.

Shall We Dance

(Original spoken word by Jill Wyckoff)

Shall we dance?
You lead.
I'll follow.
We'll swing to whatever moves us.
The rhythm of the blues that woo us.
A somber Samba. A rousing Rumba.
A tangled tango that seduces
all my excuses, and looses our feet
to the crazy, hazy, beat
of you.
How 'bout a manic Mambo?
Let's see how far we can go.
Let's drive up the heat and the beat of my heart
that rises and falls to the saucy sway
of you.
Krump, pop, lock me in a grip that flips me
upside down.
The world's on its head instead of right side up.
My view skewed to the tantalizing tune
of you.
Upside down, downside up,
twirling, whirling, spinning, breaking
under your control.

Captured in your spell as you lead so well,
to the chaotic cadence
of you.
Wait!
Stop right there!
This is the part where I cleverly slip in the fact
that this poem isn't about dancing with
with some hunky, heady, heartthrob
that captured me in his seductive spell.
No.
It's about dancing cheek-to-cheek with the
thoughts I've come to know all too well.
You know the kind I'm talking about,
those evil thoughts that keep you
stewing in the juices of pity and resentment.
The kind of thinking that has you drinking in judgments about others and
yourself
till your drunk out of your mind from
a toxic cocktail of two parts self-hatred mixed
with three parts offense, topped off with a
heaping helping of depression.
It's a noxious potion that goes down with a slow burn and leaves a bitter,
bitter, taste in your mouth.
And so now you see how the dance analogy
makes sense, right?
But then I added a drinking analogy so I've
mixed you all up now, haven't I?
Ah, but that's what happens when we entertain thoughts of destruction;
whispers from
the dark side that disguise as light.
Confusion ensues to the point where we can't

even choose a single analogy!
It's chaos and catastrophe all wrapped together,
warping our mind till we're out of our mind.
So what's a gal to do?
What's anyone to do?
Stop it.
That 's right. We've got the right to stop it.
Take back control and fight it.
Make those thoughts our prisoner.
Take them down, toss out the key.
Of course, it's not easy.
It takes grit and determination to change our thoughts about a situation.
But don't let your imagination run wild child.
Stop it!
This is what I tell myself.
And for what it's worth, you can grab it too.
Take control of those toxic thoughts
that try to take control of you.
Come on! Let's do this!
Next time our thoughts entangle in a sordid,
twisted tango and we feel we're gonna
blow our flippin' top.
Let's stop...
Have another thought.
A better one.
A brighter one.
A righter one.
And let's tell that son of a gun,
dance over.

We're DONE!

Chapter 12

Recess

THINK IT'S TIME for a little break. Breaks are pivotal for the creative. Contrary to popular belief, or our inner taskmaster, breaks are not a waste of time. They give us space to imagine, to explore, to express. They feed and nourish our souls (now *that's* food for thought).

If you've already allotted time to read this book today, then use this time to play instead.

Feel free to change into your play clothes, grab something yummy to drink and munch, and try any one or all of these. Don't forget to invite the Holy Spirit. He wants to play too.

- Write a riddle.
- Doodle.
- Paint, draw, or color a feeling. (What does a feeling look like? No one knows so you can't get it wrong.)
- Have a dance party in your kitchen (even if you're the only one dancing).
- Write a silly song and sing it into your phone's voice recorder.
- Color a picture using all the wrong colors.
- Grab a friend and do a blind taste test.
- Write a letter to someone you love.

- Find a dance workout video on YouTube and get your groove on.
- Turn on some music and draw with your non-dominant hand.
- Write a poem that rhymes.
- Write a poem that doesn't rhyme.
- Read a children's book.
- Read a children's book out loud with an accent.
- Take a walk outside. Search out beauty, and capture it with your cell phone.
- Use an app to make a collage out of your pictures.
- Find an object in your closet or junk drawer and write a short story about it.
- Close your eyes and imagine yourself where you've always dreamed of being. See how far your imagination can take you.
- Search out funny videos and memes and laugh your head off.
- Think of something to do that's not on this list.

How did that make you feel? Refreshed? Inspired? Carefree? Did it start you dreaming again of all the creative possibilities? Did you surprise yourself? Do you want to do it again? Playing with Papa is not only good for you; it's a wartime strategy against the one who is at war with you. The enemy hates when we take time to play with God because he knows it will benefit us in more ways than he can count. That's why he whispers that it's a waste of time and suggests that you have more important things to do. We know better!

Take the opportunity to carve out space in your schedule for playtime. It doesn't matter how old we are, we are all God's kids. Explore with childlike wonder and discover there's more to you than you thought.

Play.
Do the unexpected.
Take a break
from
your usual,
your typical,
your go-to.

Play.

Feel the freedom.
Now.
And again.
And again.
Until the
rhythm of the new
gets so ingrained
in you,
that freedom
becomes normal.
And play
becomes
your bliss.

Chapter 13
Come As A Child

Jesus said, *"Let the little children come to me, and do not hinder them, for the kingdom of heaven belongs to such as these."* (Matthew 19:14). He also said, *"Truly I tell you, unless you change and become like little children, you will never enter the kingdom of heaven."*

(Matthew 18:3)

WHY, THEN, ARE we trying to be so grown up all the time? I get that there isn't any benefit to acting childish, but *childlike* is a whole other story. It's what our Lord did with His Father. **Jesus went off and prayed, firm in His identity as a child of God who needed time alone with His Daddy. He didn't do anything He didn't see His Father doing or say anything He didn't hear His father saying. He was perfectly childlike, completely dependent on His Papa; postured as a Son.**

I don't know about you, but this removes any weight I put on myself to have it all together when I approach God. It's actually the exact opposite of how we're to come to Him. Like Jesus, we can approach our Papa with childlike innocence that is ours by the redemptive work on the cross.

Daddy bids you to come. The table is set. He's brought out your favorite snacks and some coloring books. He's waiting like a proud Papa with open arms and a great big smile!

Chapter 14
Just Imagine

THANKS TO FACEBOOK memories, I know that six years ago, from the exact date of this writing, my husband and I were on a *Sound of Music* tour in Salzburg, Austria. What a dream come true! As I sang and danced on the exact steps where Maria and the children sang do-re-mi (I have the video to prove it), I was immediately taken back to my childhood. The *Sound of Music* (*20th Century Fox, 1965*) was the first movie I ever saw on the big screen. My mother took me, and I will never forget coming out of the theater, dreamy-eyed. Reaching for my mom's hand, I gazed up and said with conviction, "When I grow up, I'm going to be Maria. I'm going to marry the captain and have all those children." Looking back, it's interesting that I hadn't picked up on the whole Nazi thing. All I could see was a beautiful family who sang together, loved each other, and lived happily ever after. My little girl heart dreamed of being a wife and a mother, especially a singing one. My mom's response, "Jill, you can't be Maria. We're not even catholic."

I don't think my mother purposely meant to burst my bubble, though I remember feeling rather deflated. Thankfully, it didn't stop me from continuing to imagine my life with a loving husband and lots of children. Five years later, I fell in love with another singing family— non-catholics this time. I dreamed of traveling in a multi-color painted school bus playing shows in various towns. I was no longer Maria. I was Laurie, the teenage daughter in *The Partridge Family*.

> *"Hello, world, hear the song that we're singin'*
> *C'mon get happy!*
> *A whole lot of lovin' is what we'll be bringin'*
> *We'll make you happy!*
> *We had a dream, we'd go travelin' together,*
> *We'd spread a little lovin' then we'd keep movin' on.*
> *Somethin' always happens whenever we're together*
> *We get a happy feelin' when we're singing a song."*

This was the Partridge Family theme song, *C'mon Get Happy* (Lyrics by Wes Farrell and Danny Janssen). It was my perfect dream. I imagined me and my family travelin' together, singin' a song, bringin' love and making people happy. Aaaahhh—idyllic!

When I was a child, I dreamed like a child. Everything was possible. As I got a little older and hit my tumultuous teenage years, imagination was my escape. My teachers told me to stop daydreaming. My friends told me that I lived in a fairytale world. They all thought I was silly. At the time, I thought they were right, but I couldn't help myself. Looking back, I see that it wasn't silly at all. It was what kept me sane.

Eventually, I fell in with the wrong crowd, slipped into alcohol and drugs, got married and divorced, and became a single mother. Not exactly the life I dreamed of. Little by little, my imagination took a back seat as the demands of my situation occupied most of my attention. I was either trying to figure out how to care for my small children or too tired to think at all. Imagination was for dreamers and dreamers lived in a fairytale world—not my world.

There are many things in our day-to-day life that vie for our attention. Many of us have had our dreams stolen, squashed, diminished, and devalued. We've watched helplessly as our dreams were sucked up and choked to death by our circumstances and situations. We've surrendered whatever was left of our imagination as frivolous and determined our dreams as a waste of time. But is that really true? Are they frivolous and a waste of time?

In actuality, your ability to imagine and to dream is built into your design—God wrote it into your DNA. It's necessary.

I think you would agree that our Heavenly Father, the Master Creator, has the grandest imagination of all. God is the only one who can create something out of nothing. **All creativity is birthed out of imagination—first God's, then yours. When we create, we tap into His sanctified imagination. It is neither frivolous nor useless—it is Holy.** When we dream of what could be, we enter into God's Supernatural possibilities. It's not silly at all. It's Divine.

Before He created you, He imagined you. You are, literally, His dream come true.

Our God-given ability to imagine allows us to imagine Him. He is majestic, Supernatural, beyond anything we can see or know; absolutely nothing compares to Him. We have to use our imagination to even have a yocto of an idea (one septillionth of a base unit or 0.000 000 000 000 000 000 000 001.) of how great and good and vast He is. David, in the book of Psalms, uses his imagination to describe the many thoughts God has toward us, *"Were I to count them, they would outnumber the grains of sand."* (Psalm 139:18). And John supposed (imagined) that if all the things Jesus did were written down, there wouldn't be enough room in the whole world for the number of books that would be written. (John 21:25). Imagine that!

Throughout the Bible, from the prophets of the Old Testament to Revelation in the New Testament, we see imagery, metaphor, simile, storytelling—imagination exercised creatively to reveal the magnitude of God and His Kingdom. Imagination that reveals ultimate reality.

Imagination is not just an inconsequential by-product of our humanity. It is purposed to be an essential connection with Divinity. The more we spend time with God, the more we can imagine Him. And the more we imagine Him, the more we can reveal the reality of Him through our unique creative expression.

"The Christian...is free to have imagination. This too is our heritage. The Christian is the one whose imagination should fly beyond the stars."

— Francis Schaeffer, Art and the Bible

So to recap: All creativity starts with imagination. We inherited imagination through our Father God. He designed us to imagine Him, to meditate on good things, to dream of endless possibilities and an eternity with Him.

Then why do we spend so much time imagining the worst?

Ah, there's that tricky little devil again. Whispers, subtle suggestions. Manipulation infects our imagination. The enemy can't read our mind, but he can get inside our head. Human beings aren't exactly that tricky. Satan's playbook has worked since the Garden, and he's not creative enough to think of anything new. Sadly, he doesn't have to. A spark of doubt can ignite our imaginations and take us down a path of self-destruction, if we're not careful.

Once I began to experience breakthroughs in my creative journey, I had a vision (sanctified daydream from Papa to me) of the enemy flicking seeds into my spirit when I was younger. He flicked, then walked. He didn't stick around to see what I would do with those seeds. I suppose he sensed that I would water and nurture those seeds on my own. And I did. I took such good care of those darn seeds that they grew into giant gnarly trees bursting with rotten fruit. Dried up, withered, and disgusting fruit formed from the lies the enemy planted. And I tended them with my imagination.

This rotten fruit born of my imagination became my reality. That's the power of imagination. It can be used for good: submitted to God, or for destruction: submitted to self.

I believe that now, perhaps more than ever, God is asking us to exercise our imagination. In March of this year, 2020, the whole world felt the impact of Covid-19. It seemed that overnight we entered into weeks of quarantine. Businesses, restaurants, churches, schools, travel, and events were closed down. Individuals were even prohibited from being with loved ones in the hospital and gathering for weddings and funerals. Our normal way of life was completely disrupted on nearly every level. This pandemic forced people to think of new ways of doing things, to imagine solutions that would carry us forward in a world that would never be the same. I believe those with the sharpest imaginations will be the ones carrying the torch for the rest of us. Those torches will light the way with strategies for better education, medicines that help cure diseases, music that makes us dance, and stories that inspire us to dream again. The light that shines from our imagination will light up the whole world if we give it a whirl.

My friend, Angela, is wonderfully creative in numerous ways. She shared part of her creative journey growing up as a pastor's kid in the '80s.

> I was a very imaginative child and the idea of dragons, fairies, and unicorns were always running around in my head. I loved to tell stories and draw what I saw. It wasn't until I was a little older that I was told that it was wrong of me to paint or imagine such magical things. Dragons were demonic and magical things were not of God. I was broken-hearted and felt like there was something wrong with me. Why could CS Lewis write magical stories and it was ok for him but not for me? So I developed almost two different identities. One that was valuable and important to God, and then a creative imaginative side that was invaluable. Then I went to Bethel Supernatural School of Ministry in 2001, and I had some very powerful encounters. In one of them, God set me free and told me that he loved my fantastic imagination. Ever since, it has been a priority to me to help people learn that the imagination is the very space God uses to help us see his spirit, and also give creatives a super-power to change atmospheres and cultures Nothing in the world exists that didn't first exist in the imagination of God, or in the imagination of man. Knowing this, we as creative become dangerous (in a good way) when we allow God into our imagination because then we create heaven's realities on the earth.

Maybe some of you have a similar story to Angela; you were discouraged from using your imagination. I love what Angela said about using our imaginations to become dangerous—to create heaven's realities on the earth. That is the reason we create and the reason God led you to read this book. As you use your sanctified imagination to create, you will become dangerous to the enemy and become an influence for God.

I encourage you to embrace your God-given imagination. Let it ignite your creativity. Dream with Papa and step into all of the wonders He wants to do through you. Your imagination connected with God's is the pathway to Supernatural creativity.

Imagine This:

- Close your eyes and imagine being successful in your creative journey with God.
- Journal what you imagine.

What if the
seeds
you sowed
produced
something
never seen
or experienced
before?

What would you sow?

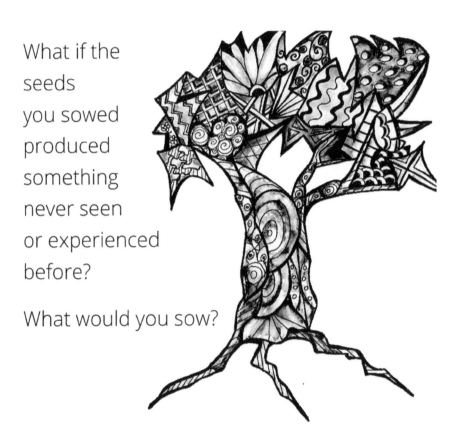

Chapter 15
Overcoming

"Just as it is written:
"For Your sake we are killed all day long;
We were regarded as sheep to be slaughtered."
But in all these things we overwhelmingly conquer
through Him who loved us."

— Romans 8:36-37 (NASB)

VERCOMING IS A process. The first step is realizing who you are. Who am I?

Pause on that question for a moment. Be still. Breathe. Meditate on it.

If you're like most people, you might be listing off the things that you do or your titles. I'm a mother, wife, teacher, truck driver, or accountant. These are all well and good, but what happens when your children grow up and leave the nest, or your spouse wants a divorce, or you lose your job? Then who are you?

What you do, your titles and functions, are how you express who you are, or rather, who you believe yourself to be.

Everything we do starts with an appropriate idea of our authentic selves, our true identity. And no matter who you are, your identity will be challenged and under attack. I love how John Eldreidge expresses it in his book, *Waking the Dead: The Secret to a Heart Fully Alive* (*Thomas Nelson*). "The story of your life is the story of the long and brutal assault on your heart by the one who knows what you could be and fears it." The Father of Lies is fully aware that you belong to God, and He has a plan to work through you. Rule #1 in the enemy's playbook: Attack their identity. "*If* you are the son of God." Insert doubt. He used this approach with Jesus in the desert, and he uses it with us.

Who am I? Only Jesus gets to answer that question. We are defined through Him and by Him.

Ask Him. Who am I to you, Lord?

On January 1, 2012, I stood in the shower sobbing at the thought of what my new year would bring. I had just come out of six months of illness, hospitals, specialists, and numerous medical tests. My condition was worsening, and there were no real answers. I was overwhelmingly discouraged thinking about all I had been through and what lay ahead. I was wallowing in grief, bitterness, and self-pity.

Feeling that I was at the end of my rope, I reached out to a prophetic Christian Life Coach who was a friend of a friend. On the way to our meeting, I remember thinking about how invisible I felt.

I recalled the line from the movie *Avatar*, "I see you," and thought to myself how wonderful it would be to be seen—*truly seen.*

That meeting changed my life. I cannot go into the depth of what transpired, but the overarching theme was about my identity. She said that God had given her a vision of what was taking place physically inside of me. She said, "Your Spirit is warring with your soul. Your Spirit knows the truth about your identity (who God created you to be), but your soul is holding on to the lies and word curses (bad things that people have said about you). This opposition, this war within, is manifesting in illness, depression, and limitation."

She then said something that blew my mind. She said, "God wants you to know you are not invisible." And then she moved closer, looked directly into my eyes, and said slowly with great passion, "God says, 'I see you. I see you. I see you.'"

As you can imagine, the floodgates opened, and there was a torrent of tears. To my absolute shock, God Himself was speaking directly to me through this woman. Only He could have known what I was thinking in the car on the way to the meeting. He saw me—*truly* saw me! He knew my pain. While I was feeling devastatingly alone in my misery, He was right there by my side. It's one thing to know it in theory; it's a whole other thing to hear it audibly. It was miraculous!

I left that meeting feeling full of life and hope. I was determined to discover my true identity and align my soul with the truth of my spirit. The first thing I did was to write a list of the lies I believed about myself. That was easy. I wrote them down, then tore them up and threw them away. Then I listened to the voice of God who "sees me" and wrote what He said about me. *I am...* I have to admit it felt strange, foreign, and even a bit boastful to write positive things about myself. But I was willing to let God transform my mind, and so I wrote. In most cases, my *I am's* were the exact opposite of the lies I believed about myself. Isn't it ironic that the very things we think are our greatest weaknesses are actually the very things we were designed for? Enemy playbook #2 revealed: the curse is the reverse!

I placed my *I am* statements all over the house, the office, the car, anywhere I could see them. I meditated on them. I spoke them out loud to myself. I figured if God could speak the world into existence, then I could speak His truth into my existence. I began to make choices based on what God said about me, my true identity, not my false one. These were very different choices, by the way, and they were not easy to make. But they led to my overcoming. They led me here to you.

I experienced great physical and emotional healing as I stepped into my identity. The civil war raging within my body ceased as my soul aligned with the truth of who God said I was.

I encourage you to take the time to talk with God. Write down the lies you've been believing about yourself, and then write what God says about you. I may not know you personally, but I know that you are creative because you're the spitting image of your Daddy God. I know that you are more than a conqueror because of who lives inside you. I know that there's a calling on your life and that you've been given everything you need to fulfill that calling because your Master Creator wrote it into your DNA. You are capable, qualified, gifted, anointed, perfectly loved, and so much more. God's word tells me so. And here's a big one (at least it was for me), I know you are worthy because Papa God loves you so much that He sent His son to die for you. Jesus makes you worthy.

As you overcome the lies of the enemy and step into the truth of who you are, God will give you opportunities to test it out. That's the fun part. Ok, and the scary part too. But it's the only way for you to discover what you can do.

Step 1: Uncover your true identity.

- Talk with God.
- Write down the lies and destroy them.
- Write your *I am* declarations and post them.
- Speak them aloud over yourself—let this truth sink into your bones.

Step 2: Step into your true identity. Walk it out.

- Look for opportunities to express the real you.
- Take them.

Remember when I went to the 24-hour worship in the wee hours of the morning to paint in public? I wrestled with that decision. I didn't feel confident in my abilities, but God helped me (over time) to step into the truth of who He created me to be. *I am* brave; my confidence is in Him. *I am* gifted uniquely, so there's no need to compare. Yes, stepping in was uncomfortable, but it was where reality became cemented.

Identity is actualized on the front lines.

Eventually, you will find your front line experiences becoming more manageable—enjoyable even. Don't get used to it. Just when you think about settling into your easy chair, God will redecorate. He's not interested in your comfort. He's interested in your transformation. His will is to elevate you to your next level, to stretch you into another area of your design, another front line, glory to ever-increasing glory.

A year or two after I started my painting journey, several of us from our church were caravaning from San Diego to Sierra Vista, Arizona, where our pastors were doing a prophetic conference. Brae and I were going to support our pastors and pray for people at the conference. About 4 hours into a 7-½ hour drive our pastor messaged us that each of us were going to be leading a session at the conference. I almost had a heart attack! That was the last thing on earth I ever thought I could do, but there was no turning back now. As you can imagine, I stressed out for the entire trip. I could barely eat, think, sleep, or socialize. I was a mess. Thankfully, my pastor gave us the opportunity to choose a topic that we were passionate about. I had already had breakthrough with stepping into my painting journey, so I chose the topic "Just do it." Ironic, since in this new assignment, I certainly didn't feel equipped to "do" anything. But I did. I walked it out. In the last session of the conference, I encouraged attendees with what I had previously experienced in my creative journey and what I was currently walking out (afraid, but "just doing it"). And because I met the challenges head-on, God met me on the front lines. He gave me the authority to speak boldly and activate attendees in walking out their own authority as children of God imbued with the power of the Holy Spirit.

"That which does not kill us makes us stronger."
— Friedrich Nietzsche

I thought it would kill me. It didn't. Instead, this experience launched me into public speaking, which eventually became very enjoyable. I don't know why I doubted. God knew it was part of my design all along. And so did my Pastor. He had eyes to see what I couldn't yet see.

It is vitally important to have people in our lives who see us the way God sees us. Sometimes these people will be family or close friends; they may be coworkers or church leaders, counselors, or coaches. Your first thought might be to reject their words of encouragement as bias or flattery. But God uses these people to steer us in the right direction. For me, God used Pastor Craig Muster to lovingly but firmly kick my bootie into gear. Craig continued to open doors of opportunity. He pushed back when I balked. He affirmed my calling and pulled the gold out of me. I will forever be grateful for his persistent nudging and loving leadership. God used him to help me grow up. Now He's using me to help others grow up. It is a sign and a wonder. It is magnificently humbling.

Forewarned is forearmed, so heed this warning. The Mocker won't stop mocking. That's his job. Whenever God reveals another facet of your original design, even though you know the truth, the Mocker will try to convince you otherwise.

When I began speaking in public, I did not realize that it would lead to preaching at our church. By this time, I had gotten a bit more comfortable, and I knew it was part of my design. But the old comparison thing reared its ugly head once again.

God: "It's time for you to preach."

Me: "God, how can I preach? Pastor Karlet is so freakin powerful. There's no way I can be like her!

God: "I don't want you to be like her. I want you to be like you."

Honestly, if you saw Pastor Karlet Muster preach, you'd feel the same. She's a brilliant, passionate, powerhouse of a preacher who barely looks at her notes. As soon as she opens her mouth, you're captivated by the rich timbre of her voice, which easily projects God's truth across a crowded room even without a microphone. And if you think her speaking is amazing, you should hear her sing. She's magnificent! She's a hard act to follow, to say the least. But when God told me that He wanted me to be like me, it released the pressure I put on myself (thanks to the Mocker) to be like her. Of course, I had already learned from my process as a creative that it was impossible to be like someone else, but I needed it reinforced in this new situation.

The fact is, I have a very different preaching style than Pastor Karlet; not better or worse, just different. I am *me*. I am passionate about Jesus yet somewhat quirky, often dramatic, and rather humorous (if I do say so myself). Once it sunk in that I don't have to try to be something I'm not, all the weight dropped off. I felt completely comfortable because, after all, I was just being myself. Take it or leave it.

Our goal shouldn't be to try to get people to like us but to walk out our revelation of our design while at the same time pursuing greater revelation.

If I had not risked taking the opportunity to preach, I would not have discovered my love for it, and in fact, that I was born for it.

The same is true for my discovering that I love to paint, write, do spoken word, act, teach, lead, coach. Most recently, during this pandemic, I learned that I enjoy doing live-stream videos. Who'd have thought?! If you had asked me years ago if I would be doing any of these things, I would have laughed my head off, "No way! You've been sipping the crazy juice!"

But God.

Step 3: Give away what you've received so others can be blessed.

If I had stayed painting in the comfort of my own home where no one would see, I would have missed out on God moving in countless ways to restore people's lives through my paintings. If I had not stretched to Gumbie proportions and taken the opportunities to speak in public, teach, and preach, I would not have seen God work many miracles in and through people's lives. I would have missed out on what has become my most favorite thing in life, my absolute bliss; to see others awaken to the truth of who God says they are and step into their assignments. The very thought makes me want to weep.

"Freely you received, freely give."
— Matthew 10:8 (NASB)

Your breakthroughs will come as you press into intimacy with the Lord. Let Him lead you.

Your Heavenly Father has so much more He wants to reveal. **The** more you learn about God, the more you'll discover about yourself. The chrysalis of self-doubt and false identity will not be able to contain you any longer.

As you overcome old habitual thinking and walk in ever-increasing fullness, even your physical body will respond. For years it was believed that 97 percent of our DNA had no function. Scientists called it "junk DNA." But as my mom used to say, "God doesn't make junk." In fact, these DNA molecules are now regarded as treasures, because they actually increase the ability of the organism to evolve. They turn off old genes that are not needed any longer and turn on new ones.

> "Therefore if anyone is in Christ, this person is a new creation; the old things passed away; behold, new things have come."
>
> — 2 Corinthians 5:17 (NASB)

My friend, behold, you are in every way a new creation. You were created to overcome and become the manifestation of your original design—who you were always created to be—the real you. This is your metamorphosis moment. You are destined to fly.

Chapter 16
To Be Or Not To Be

As Directors of *Kingdom Writers Association*, my husband and I have often been asked the question, "If I haven't experienced complete breakthrough in my personal life, should I stop writing my story?" This is a valid question, and some might advise otherwise. But we feel that it is good to write. Unless it causes you great distress, *write your story*. Ask God to meet you right there in the middle of the page in the midst of your pain. Maybe it will look more like journaling. Maybe it will take the form of an Epic Fantasy or a children's book. Whatever it looks like, trust God to guide you.

But—and this is a very big BUT—do not release your writing out into the world until you have worked through your healing. Write it all out, gain your breakthrough and then go back and retool it for redemptive and restorative impact. Our work is meant to carry messages of transformation, hope, and healing; bring light into dark places. This is our calling as Kingdom creatives.

I propose that this is a good pathway for all of our various creative expressions. We create because we cannot help but do so. We are creative beings, and we know that creativity is healing. Don't stop creating. God can and will meet you as you do. He will take you on a wonderful journey of transformation so that you can create with Him and for Him—your breakthrough leading to breakthrough for others.

Section 3

The Call To Restorative Impact

Chapter 17
God's Creative Army

W E ARE PART of God's massive army of creatives, called to the front lines to create works and innovate ideas that advance His Kingdom. In Revelation 11:15, we see what His Kingdom will look like, "*The kingdom of the world has become the kingdom of our Lord and of his Messiah. He will rule for ever and ever.*"

When we pray, "Your Kingdom come, Your will be done on earth as it is in heaven," we are asking Him to come and believing that He will. Regardless of whether or not He will come in our lifetime, we need to prepare for His arrival. We want to see the kingdoms of this world become the Kingdoms of our God, and one of the ways this will happen is through God's creative army.

Presently, the kingdoms of this world are in an uproar. I don't need to tell you how dark it is but suffice it to say that we are seeing some of the signs of the times that Jesus told his disciples about in Matthew 24.

This isn't the first time our world has been in an upheaval. In Zechariah 1, God tells the prophet Zechariah to tell the people that He's angry with them. He says in verses 3 and 4, "'*Return to me,' declares the Lord Almighty, 'and I will return to you,' says the Lord Almighty. Do not be like your ancestors, to whom the earlier prophets proclaimed: This is what the Lord Almighty says: 'Turn from your evil ways and your evil practices.'*" (NIV)

Here God is very angry with His people, but as we read further, He promises to show mercy and declares that he will rebuild. *"My towns will again overflow with prosperity, and the Lord will again comfort Zion and choose Jerusalem."* (v. 17)

How does He do this? That's the exciting part!

The angel of the Lord appears to Zechariah in a vision and shows him four horns. These are the horns that scattered Judah, Israel, and Jerusalem so that no one could raise their head. Like today, people were caught in the web of self-destruction, devastation, hopelessness. They were too stuck in this web to look up into the eyes of God and see their salvation. Then the Angel of the Lord showed Zechariah four craftsmen.

Zechariah asked, *"What are these coming to do?"* (v. 21)

"He answered, 'These are the horns that scattered Judah so that no one could raise their head, but the craftsmen have come to terrify them and throw down these horns of the nations who lifted up their horns against the land of Judah to scatter its people.'" (v. 21)

God's answer to a godless kingdom, in Zechariah's time and now, is His craftsmen—His creatives. We are his mighty warriors. He is calling us to the front lines to *terrify* the enemy through creative expression!

Our creativity, in collaboration with the Holy Spirit, brings righteousness; life as it should be according to God's standard. We are living in a culture of confusion. God is using creativity as a weapon of mass destruction to bring clarity and redemption. Through Him, our creative expression becomes restorative in nature: "having the ability to restore health, strength, or a feeling of well-being." (Google dictionary) **Our creative expressions, imbued with the power of the Holy Spirit, have the power to save, heal, deliver, transform, reform, and restore. Its universal language breaks down barriers, provokes thought, inspires, enlightens, and sets a table for God to come in and dine.** Throughout history, we've seen the power of creativity to shape society and shift cultures. Creativity under the influence of the Holy Spirit always points to the one true God and has the power to advance the Kingdom of heaven on earth. And *that*, my friends, terrifies the enemy.

I love this quote by Matt Tommey. He's using the words artists and art here, but the same is true for all creatives regardless of the expression. "Artists are the life-givers in culture. We are a pivotal intersection point where the Kingdom of Heaven meets culture. It is there that we have the unique opportunity, through the power of the Holy Spirit, to translate the Kingdom of Heaven into a language that bypasses words and goes directly into the human spirit. When we collaborate with the Holy Spirit in this dance of Kingdom creativity, His power, His Life, and His Light merge with our faith, creative thoughts, imaginations, desires, and skill into art that carries the literal presence and power of God. It is in this context that our art, no matter the creative medium becomes prophetic."

You are being called to join God's army of creatives.

You are God's chosen people,
created to create without hesitation
for every tribe, every nation
to affect all generations.
Pulling from the unseen into the seen
to generate art that is a prophecy.
Your creativity, no matter the expression,
is the representation of God's celebration
over his creation.
Life-giving, righteous living, radical, empirical,
lyrical love that knows no limits and often colors outside the lines
to define a lifeline to the vine that connects directly to the father's
heart.
God calls you to terrify the enemy through beauty, through
ingenuity;
shifting cultures, shaping worldviews,
making Jesus famous in the news.

That's the role of the artist
and possibly the hardest thing to remember
is that it's not just about having a gift, or a talent or a skill,
but the will to do God's will without saying you won't or don't
because you think you can't.
Because you can.
You were designed for it, called to it, and you can do it.
Not on your own, of course, but you don't have to. God imbued you
with His Spirit,
the power to act and to do. And together you
are meant to spread His righteousness through
your creative pursuits.
Now don't get me wrong, that devil is mean and he'll try to make
you believe that:
It's a waste of time.
You've got nothing to give.
Everyone's better than you.
Your style is odd.
It won't appeal to the masses.
It will never sell.
It looks like hell
And, well…
you get the drill.
The devil isn't a genius.
He can't even create a good lie,
he just spreads around the same ones
because he can't create
so he intimidates and instigates and hopes that we'll take the bait.
Oftentimes, we do.
But no more.

I prophesy now that you will not bow down to the lies and compromise all that God is going to do through you. You will rise up, knowing your identity full well and you will create expressions that hold the key to setting men free in the marketplace and in the streets, not only the church.

You are part of an army of creatives. Change agents for God. Creativity is your worship, your weapon and your superpower. Today is the day, this is the hour for you to take your place, press on toward the goal to win the prize for the upward calling in Jesus Christ.

If you agree, shout amen!

Chapter 18
Inside Out

I T IS AN amazing feeling to discover that God created you to create and that He equipped you for that purpose. It's blissful to explore what the Master Creator put inside you and then be able to express this in a way that is beautiful, powerful, strategic, and/or innovative. This process is not static. It continues to grow and expand as God leads us from glory to glory, and we submit our will to His. This is a journey where the Lord brings what is inside of us out to affect the world around us.

Why?

God intends to touch the hearts of humankind through creativity. He has a plan to do so through us; His army of creatives. Our mission is clear:

> "And Jesus came up and spoke to them, saying, 'All authority in heaven and on earth has been given to Me. Go, therefore, and make disciples of all the nations, baptizing them in the name of the Father and the Son and the Holy Spirit, teaching them to follow all that I commanded you; and behold, I am with you always, to the end of the age.'"

> — Matthew 28:18-20 (NASB)

We've got a job to do. Every Christian has been called to this Great Commission. We can be assured that God has given us authority to make disciples of all nations, and He is with us as we do. We have been designed and equipped for this purpose. In the past, many believed that the only way to do this was to hand out tracts or stand on a street corner with a sign that read, "Turn or Burn." God is showing us, perhaps now more than ever, that there are many ways to reach the lost and disciple them into the Kingdom. To be clear, the Word does not change, nor does the message of the Gospel of Jesus Christ, but the delivery method looks different from person to person. How so? Each of us expresses the Gospel through our unique voice, imagination, and experience—our one-of-a-kind fingerprints. It's the same story told differently, by design. In this way, we can reach different people groups and impact our own spheres of influence. God's detail for diversity is nothing short of a sign and a wonder. And because you and I carry His message uniquely, it releases you to be you and me to be me to the fullest that we can be—for HIM.

God's army of creatives have been given the authority to reach their communities for Christ with revelation expressed through creativity. When we collaborate with the Holy Spirit, we take His thoughts and make them visible through our creative expression, bringing the unseen into the seen to create works and innovations that are prophetic in nature.

> *"The artisan puts flesh on the work of the Spirit and makes that reality visible for others to experience."*
> — Christ John Otto

God prophesies His nature through us in this co-mission to reach the lost next door or across the nations. It's brilliantly strategic.

Marc Dupont of Mantle of Praise Ministries puts it this way,

In short, prophetic creativity is art and creative expression that essentially does two things. One, it speaks of something else, especially something greater- such as the reality of the person of God, eternal truths, or the purposes of God. It speaks into both the now and the emerging of eternity. Secondly, prophetic creativity due to the freshness, the excellence, and quite possibly the mystery of the creativity draws the viewer, or listener, into the examination of its sublime and oft hidden message. In a real sense, prophetic creativity is much like healings and miracles when they become a sign and wonder. Because prophetic creativity speaks of a future relationship, or a future thing to come, as opposed to a static truth, it tends to be alive, anointed, and/or prophetic.

Years ago, when I painted that prayer for Joe (see Chapter 3), I did not realize my painting titled "Out of the Ashes" was a prophetic decree that would one day be manifested in his life. Likewise, I had no idea that the abstract painting I painted in an Austrian park in 2014 was a prophetic word that a woman named Gertrude had received for healing three years prior. I now know that God works prophetically through my creativity, regardless of whether or not I'm aware of it. As long as I'm partnering with Him, His prophetic voice will be heard and it will capture the heart of the one (or the many) that it is intended for. The same is true for you.

I've taught many prophetic creativity workshops and conducted numerous Creative Awakenings retreats. I've been blessed to see many of the participants experience deep healing and transformation from God as he encountered them through a creative exercise. One of my favorite exercises is to have participants paint with their eyes closed. It removes the individual's natural agenda and their need to control the outcome. Instead, they experience God's agenda, His prophetic voice speaking directly to their heart. It's like a kiss from their Papa. Before we start, we invite the Holy Spirit to paint with us and guide our hands. We make room for Him to move. Afterwards, participants take a few moments to observe their painting; colors, movement, and any random shapes that emerge. They ask God for revelation, "Lord, what are you saying to me through this?" From there, we share the paintings with one another to see if God gives revelation through someone else.

Oftentimes, the individual is blown away by what they discover and we are all undone by how Papa blesses each one of His children so uniquely. There are lots of tears and lots of tissues as we slobber and snot our way through each revelation.

I have so many testimonies about this, but one of my favorites is with a woman I'll call June. She was brought to one of my retreats by a friend and seemed a little unsure about being there. June is a brilliant artist but hadn't fully accepted that about herself. This exercise was a bit out of her comfort zone, but she was a good sport about it. Afterwards, June shared her painting. She was a little discouraged that she hadn't really heard from God. But when she showed it to the others, they all saw something in it that was beautiful and meaningful to her. After everyone else shared, I expressed what God was showing me. Now to be clear, these blind paintings aren't very detailed or defined; it helps to look at them with "soft eyes" and ask the Holy Spirit for revelation. As soon as I looked at her painting, it struck me how obvious it was. "I see you. It's you getting out of the boat. Just like Peter, you're out of the boat." At this point, she looked at her friend as if she'd seen a ghost, and the whole group held their collective breaths waiting to hear why.

That morning when everyone arrived, I gave each person a journal and asked them to write down their hopes and expectations for the retreat. In absolute shock, June shared her journal entry with the group, "Lord, I want to get out of the boat."

God met June in the deepest desire of her heart. He put His hand on hers, and together they painted a prophecy that changed the trajectory of her life.

God's prophetic voice comes in every size, shape, and color. It defies logic and deftly outmaneuvers our propensity to stuff it in the itty-bitty box of our own expectations. When we let Him put His hand on ours and create with us, our creative expressions carry His voice to their intended audience and draws them closer to His heart. In this way, everything we create with him becomes a powerful tool for outreach; to prophesy and evangelize.

"Therefore, we are ambassadors for Christ, as though God were making an appeal through us;"

— 2 Corinthians 5:20 (NASB)

As ambassadors for Christ, we preach through our creative expression. Through words, paintings, dance, sculpture, music, ideas, solutions, and so on; every expression of our sanctified imagination. There are no limits because God has no limits.

It may be unusual to think of God preaching through creativity. But He does it all day, every day. Psalm 19:1 *"The heavens declare the glory of God; the skies proclaim the work of his hands."* God is displayed through the work of His hands and the work of ours when we are willing to collaborate with Him.

Did you know that God can lead someone to Christ through a painting?

Dianne Tylski is a wonderful San Diego artist who discovered her calling around the age of 69. She is an evangelist and a prayer warrior who loves to take her creative talents to the streets and see God do His thing. Now in her early 70's she travels around the world to bring the Gospel message through creative means.

A few years ago, Dianne asked a number of artists in the region to paint their version of "resurrection life" and submit a photograph along with a prophetic word about the piece. It was near Easter when she set up a display in a local park with framed photographs and multiple copies of the prophetic words for each. In large lettering on the display were the words, "ART SPEAKS." When people walked by, she encouraged them to pick out a painting that resonated with them. When they pointed to the photograph, she would then read the artist's prophetic word to the person. Throughout the day, people were getting healed and touched in powerful ways as God's prophetic voice, through the artists, encountered them. Dianne related to me that on one occasion, a teenage girl chose my painting. Though fairly abstract in nature, it appealed to her and moved her in a way that she could not describe. Dianne read her the prophetic word I had written and then handed her a copy for her to keep.

He drew me out of darkness.
He wooed me into His Light.
He bathed me in His Love.
I will never be the same.
He sacrificed all to give me everything.
In Him, I am worthy.
In Him, I have hope.
In Him, I have destiny.
He sees me.
He knows me.
He loves me.

It turned out that this simple prophetic poem expressed exactly what she was feeling but had no words to express. The presence of God met her right there at that moment. Tears ran down her cheeks as the Lord ministered to her and brought her into His waiting arms. With Diane lovingly leading the way, she willingly accepted Jesus as her Lord and Savior.

This painting will never hang in a museum or sell for a million dollars. It certainly will not appeal to everyone. But for this young girl, it was a matter of life and death, and to me, that makes it priceless.

This is what it looks like to be in God's creative army on the front lines of winning souls. It's glorious.

Front Line Realities:

- Close your eyes and imagine winning souls, healing the sick, setting people free through your creative expression. Dream big. What would that look like?
- Write down what you imagine in your journal.
- Pray into it.
- Think of one small way you can use your creative expression to reach out. Start with a simple baby step. Make it attainable. Plan a course of action, give yourself a timeline, and move on it.
- Continue taking those small, sustainable baby steps toward outreach and see how God shows up. Don't be discouraged if He doesn't show up as you expect. Every step is leading you to greater maturity as you persist.
- Journal the journey.

He drew me out
of darkness.

He wooed me
into His Light.

He bathed me
in His Love.

I will never
be the same.

He sacrificed all
to give me
everything.

In Him, I am worthy.
In Him, I have hope.
In Him, I have destiny.

He sees me.
He knows me.
He loves me.

Chapter 19
Give It Up

REGARDLESS OF WHETHER you think you've got it all together and are fully capable of doing what you're called to do, or you believe you aren't the least bit qualified, your starting point is the exact same—total surrender.

Here's why.

When we think we're fully capable, there's a tendency to move on our own. We think, "I got this." And while this is partly true, at our best we will be able to produce great work but not God work. Don't get me wrong, God loves our bold confidence, but He can do infinitely more than we can ask or imagine when we surrender our will and allow His power to work through us. (Ephesians 3:20)

On the flip side, when God gives us something we believe to be way beyond our capabilities, it's because he's highlighting an area of our design we've yet to discover. He's calling us to trust Him, surrender our fears and step into His faithfulness. You can be confident that He who began a good work in you will see it through to completion (Philippians 1:6). God won't leave you hanging. That's the beauty of this unparalleled partnership with your Master Creator.

Bottom line: No matter where you are on the confidence spectrum, give it up—get over yourself—surrender your ways to His. In order to produce Supernatural creativity, you have to partner with our Supernatural God.

Try this:

- Close your eyes and imagine you and Jesus walking casually side-by-side. Ask Him to highlight an area that He'd like you to surrender and then imagine yourself placing that area into His hands. There isn't any condemnation in His eyes as He smiles at you and gladly receives it.

- Now imagine Him wanting to give you something in exchange. Hold out your hands to receive it.

- What did you give up? What did you receive in return? Journal this experience.

- When you are tempted to take back what you surrendered, look back at your journal entry and recall this visualization.

Chapter 20
Eyes To See And Ears To Hear

"For this people's heart has grown callous; they hardly hear with their ears, and they have closed their eyes. Otherwise they might see with their eyes, hear with their ears, understand with their hearts, and turn, and I would heal them.' But blessed are your eyes because they see, and your ears because they hear."

— Matthew 13:15-16 (NIV)

Your eyes and ears are blessed because they see and hear. I remember hearing this scripture when we were first learning about the power of the Holy Spirit. I suppose I always knew, instinctively, that God spoke to people, but I hadn't experienced Him speaking to me. At least, not that I knew of. I desperately wanted to have the kind of eyes and ears that were blessed. One particular Sunday, it hit me so hard that I couldn't even worship. The worship team was playing, I was standing with the rest of the congregation, but I couldn't sing. All I could do was close my eyes and beg God to let me have eyes to see and ears to hear Him. I repeated over and over in my mind, "God, I want to have ears to hear you." At one point in the middle of my silent prayer, I felt a hand rest on my shoulder. I could hear a woman's voice softly singing near me, but I didn't feel any pressure to see who it was or to stop what I was doing. I continued to press in to God, "I want so much to hear you. Lord, give me ears to hear." Within a few minutes, the worship team concluded, and in that moment of silence, the woman leaned close to my ear and said, "God says you hear more than you think you do."

Drop the mic.

I had never met this woman; she knew nothing about me, and she certainly couldn't have known what I was thinking. It was God, Himself, speaking through her. He told me unequivocally that I hear more than I think I do.

I believe we all hear more than we think we do. God's Word tells us that he who is of God hears God (John 8:47). Jesus tells us that His sheep hear His voice (John 10:27). It's as simple as that. We're the ones who complicate things. Perhaps it's because we expect Him to speak in a certain way. We put limits on His communication methods. Or maybe we disregard it as our own voice or our imagination.

From the moment I heard God tell me that I do hear Him, I started listening differently—more acutely. I raised my internal antenna. I tuned in to His frequency by reading His Word and discovering the many ways He speaks. Before I take a look at some of these ways, let's talk about why it's so important for us as His creatives to have ears to hear and eyes to see what He is doing and saying. It is vital because it's the difference between a creative who is self-sufficient and one who is Kingdom-minded—creativity that expresses God's agenda rather than our own.

> *"Therefore Jesus answered and was saying to them, 'Truly, truly, I say to you, the Son can do nothing of Himself, unless it is something He sees the Father doing; for whatever the Father does, these things the Son also does in the same way.'"*
>
> — John 5:19 (NASB)

Jesus, the Son of God, is our model. He was extremely creative, expressing through carpentry, masterful storytelling, and even one time as a vintner. His wine-making abilities are unparalleled! He created in direct connection with the source of all creativity, His Father. As such, His words and works carried the purpose and power of almighty God. **When we create out of relationship with our Heavenly Father, intersected with His Spirit, we submit our words and works to His direction and give Him room to move in purpose and supernatural power.**

Our Master Creator is, not surprisingly, creative in the way He speaks to us. Here are just a few ways, along with several scriptures.

The Word:

- Rev 3: 6 (MSG) *"Are your ears awake? Listen. Listen to the Wind Words, the Spirit blowing through the churches."*
- Hebrews 4:12 (NASB) *"For the word of God is living and active, and sharper than any two-edged sword, even penetrating as far as the division of soul and spirit, of both joints and marrow, and able to judge the thoughts and intentions of the heart."*

Seeing/Visions/Dreams (day & night visions):

- Gen 15:1 (NASB) *"After these things the word of the LORD came to Abram in a vision, saying, "Do not fear, Abram, I am a shield to you; Your reward shall be very great."*
- Daniel 2:18 (NIV) *"Then the mystery was revealed to Daniel in a night vision. Then Daniel blessed the God of heaven;*

Additionally, there are those who have heard the audible voice of the Lord; but I think more often than not, we have a sensing or a knowing in our spirit. And of course, there are times when we hear a voice in our mind that sounds like us. It may be a random thought or not something we would typically say. Sometimes when I paint, I just sense a color. Could it be me imagining things? Certainly. But (a) I believe God speaks through sanctified God-directed imagination, and (b) God knows my heart. I've asked to hear Him, and I have also asked Him to redirect me if I'm wrong. I don't stress over it. Afterall, I'm His daughter. I trust that my ears are blessed to hear Him. I don't argue or try to rationalize what I'm hearing; I just go with it. Now to be clear, I'm simply painting here. I'm not making major life decisions. If that were the case, I would certainly press in for a bit more confirmation. But when I'm creating, and I hear/sense green, I paint green, even if I've already put orange and yellow on my palette. I trust Him to lead me, even if I make mistakes along the way.

I've experienced God speaking in many other ways, and I know there are many more that I've yet to discover. He has spoken to me through bumper stickers, street signs, sounds, numbers, feathers, colors, fashion, paintings, music, film, animals, birds, nature, you name it. I'm always in awe. And because He knows me so well, He speaks in ways that appeal to me—*speaking my language* as it were. He speaks your language too.

One of the most unusual ways I've heard of God speaking is through the turning signals in my husband's car. He was on his way to work and prayed to hear God speak to him. He shut off his car radio and drove for a bit. Nothing. God was silent. Then, as he waited at the traffic light a block from his office, he became acutely aware of the sound of his turning signal. It had never struck him this way before, but it was as if it was saying two, ten, two, ten, two, ten, over and over. "How odd," he thought. Then he heard a voice in his head say, "Look it up." He drove to the office, parked his car, grabbed his NIV Bible, and stared at it blankly, trying to figure out where to even start. He ended up tossing it on the passenger seat in frustration, and it opened to 1 Thessalonians 2:10, "*You are witnesses, and so is God, of how holy, righteous and blameless we were among you who believed.*" He thought that was really cool but felt there was more. He wondered if he should go forward or backward and felt like he should go back one book. He read Colossians 2:10, then felt to turn back one more book. He ended up reading chapter 2, verse 10 in four consecutive books before the Spirit lifted, and he knew the message was complete. This is what God said through his blinkers:

"You are witnesses, and so is God, of how holy, righteous and blameless we were among you who believed."

— 1 Thessalonians 2:10

"and in Christ you have been brought to fullness. He is the head over every power and authority."

— Colossians 2:10

" that at the name of Jesus every knee should bow, in heaven and on earth and under the earth,"

— Philippians 2:10

"For we are God's handiwork, created in Christ Jesus to do good works, which God prepared in advance for us to do."

— Ephesians 2:10

This message came to Brae at the beginning of our walk with the Holy Spirit and has directed us ever since. By the way, in the days that followed, Brae checked 2:10 in every other book of the Bible. Nothing came close to having the same impact. God's message may have been delivered in an unusual way, but it was clear.

God speaks in big ways, small ways, and creative ways. He will reveal more and more to us as we set our eyes on Him, seek to hear Him, and give Him room to speak in our lives.

Tune in to God's Frequency:

- Invite God to open your ears and eyes with a greater capacity to hear and see and know His will for you and your creative expression.
- Search in scriptures for the many ways God speaks to us (don't forget to include Balaam's donkey—that's a good one!)
- Exercise your hearing/seeing skills:

  o Ask God to give you a word or two for your day (red sweater, chihuahua...etc)
  o Write the word(s) down
  o Be on the lookout for those words to appear at some point during that day
  o Don't give up if you don't see them at first. Think of it like developing a muscle. Take the opportunity to play with God and keep exercising each day.
  o Journal your experiences.
  o Invite God to speak into your creative projects and trust that He is.
  o Keep tuned in to His frequency and be prepared to be amazed.

I reflect upon the Word
the whirling
that swirls around me
beckoning
reckoning
checking
my spirit
Holy Spirit
Go deeper
search for truth
amidst lies
the false
appearing real
the deal
is to reflect
ponder
search
meditate
initiate
God's Word
and reflect
dive
reach
know
Go slow
   but go
      reflect

Chapter 21
Community

"Creativity thrives in community."

— *Diana Glyer*

IN JANUARY OF 2016, God told my husband, "*Gather My scribes and give me room to speak to them.*" Brae and I put a notice on Facebook for anyone in the San Diego area who felt called by the Lord to be a writer. We invited them to gather with us and talk about writing for the Kingdom. Our humble beginning started with five people— three ladies, Brae, and me. The following month we met again and doubled in size. We were elated! We grew bit by bit, and in July of that same year, we put on a Kingdom Writers Conference with the author of *The Shack*, William Paul Young, as our keynote speaker. After the conference, many others started coming to our monthly gathering, some driving as long as two hours to join us. It was at that point we realized we had "a thing," and so we named this thing *Kingdom Writers Association* (*KWA*).

Since then, we've increased in number and expanded via online access to include members from across America and the nations. We've launched our first two *KWA* chapters in Southern Oregon and Boise,

Idaho, and look forward to seeing *KWA* chapters crop up around the globe.

KWA's mission is to "Encourage, equip, and empower scribes to pursue their creative destinies and to publish award-winning material across all genres with the purpose of reaching more people for Christ." To this end, we've seen many people come to *KWA* with a dream to write and then have their dream come true as they hold their first published book in their hands.

When God called Brae to gather His scribes and give Him room to speak, He was calling him first and foremost to create a gathering—a community. This is the most powerful aspect of *KWA*. We are a community of writers and would-be writers who have a common goal to write with God and for God. Brae and I are not the only ones doing the encouraging. They encourage one another. It's a beautiful thing to behold. It's Kingdom.

> *"For where two or three have gathered together in My name, I am there in their midst."*
> — Matthew 18:20 (NASB)

One of our guest speakers, author Mark Stibbe, once remarked, "Our finest revelations come to us not in monologue but in dialogue. We are at our best in community, not in isolation. We do the work in isolation but we all need a CS Lewis and a Tolkien in our world who can speak into our manuscripts; help us tear things up without feeling like we're tearing up our souls in the process. I don't think we can fulfill our true destiny and potential as writers unless we go down that route. No one person's got it all together, but altogether we've got it."

This is true whether you're a writer or a weaver. **All creatives need each other. They need to be amongst their people; those who can encourage them to stay the course; those who inspire them to go to their next level. You may have heard it said that isolation is the devil's playground. If that's true, and I believe from experience that it is, then the opposite must also be true. Community is God's playground.**

God the Father, Son, Spirit, is all about relationships. In the Garden of Eden, God walked with us in perfect community. He desires to be with us and for us to be with one another.

It's not about dependence. It's about interdependence.

Another *KWA* guest speaker, Diana Glyer, spoke about the community that JRR Tolkien and CS Lewis created, *The Inklings*. This group of educated men met weekly in Oxford, England, for 17 years to talk about their writing. Two of the most notable, Tolkien and Lewis, became two of the most famous and successful authors of all time.

How important is community? Diana shared a story about JRR Tolkien being discouraged after writing his very successful children's book, *The Hobbit*. His publishers pressed him to write a sequel, but he was having a very difficult time. Tolkien shared his predicament with fellow Inkling, CS Lewis, and told him that he was going to give up. After listening, Lewis told him that he knew what the problem was. He said, "Hobbits are only interesting when they're in un-hobbit-like situations." Taking this to heart, that night, Tolkien wrote a sinister black rider on a black stallion into his story. He introduced a threat in the narrative, which unfolded into a grand un-hobbit-like adventure and resulted in the third best-selling book of all time, *The Lord of the Rings*.

"As iron sharpens iron, so one person sharpens another."
— Proverbs 27:17 (NASB)

For a number of years now, we've seen God move powerfully in San Diego regarding the community within the family of believers. Worship leaders from across the county have come together to encourage one another, collaborate together and create multi-church worship events. Pastors from many churches gather together to pray and support each other. I've been a part of artist collectives, prayer, prophetic, healing, and outreach communities that have consisted of people in all walks of life from numerous churches and ministries across the county. I have met wonderful friends that I never would have met had it not been for these communities. This has transformed our Connecticut-size County of San Diego into a much smaller community, creating fellowship, unity, support, brotherhood—a family. It has also served to eradicate comparison and competition as we come together to advance God's agenda. When He wins, we all win.

Kingdom Communities:

- Research like-minded communities in your area.
- Check out our Kingdom Creativity and Kingdom Writers communities: www.KingdomCreativityInternational.com and www.KingdomWritersAssociation.com
- Consider starting a community. Don't be afraid to start small. Where two or more or gathered in His name, there He is in the midst.

Chapter 22
Collaboration

N 2018, I danced my way up to the stage at our San Diego Kingdom Creativity Conference to the opening number from *The Greatest Showman* (*20th Century Fox*) played at a near unhealthy volume. It took some people off guard (though not the ones who know me well), and they stared at me a bit slack-jawed. But there were a few people (other than the ones I convinced beforehand) courageous enough to join the fun and dance at their seats. I made quite an entrance if I do say so myself!

When the music faded, I asked how many in the audience had seen *The Greatest Showman*. Many people raised their hands. Then I asked who had seen it more than once, twice, thrice. Fewer and fewer people raised their hands. Then I asked how many had seen it 11 times, and I was the only one with my hand up. It's true. I had seen that movie 11 times and even more since. I loved everything about it: the storyline, the acting, cinematography, transitions, costumes, music, singing, and dancing. And because I'm a diehard fan, I stayed through to the very end of the credits and was pleasantly surprised to discover a note from the director. In his directorial debut, Michael Gracey shared the following, "The making and authorized distribution of this film supported over 15,000 jobs and involved hundreds of thousands of work hours."

It took more than 15,000 people to make this movie happen, every one of them lending their unique strengths and talents to carry out the vision. And though we didn't see 98% of them, every voice mattered.

Supernatural creativity is not a one-man show. First and foremost, we collaborate with the Holy Spirit. Then God brings others to lend their strengths and support to the vision. Some are called to create on a larger scale, some much smaller. Whether large or small, overtly obvious or covertly inconspicuous, all will require some form of collaboration—even if it's simply a friend who cheers you on and encourages you to achieve your goals.

Sometimes we are the ones stewarding the vision and inviting others into it. There are seasons when we are the ones helping someone else achieve their vision. Both positions are vitally important and absolutely necessary for God's plan to affect people through creative expression. It's not about *me,* it's about *we,* because our foundation is *Thee.*

God, Himself, is the perfect model. In the beginning, God, the Father had a vision and created it, but He didn't do it by Himself. Jesus Christ, The Word, was with Him and the Spirit of God, the Holy Spirit, moved over the waters. God the Father, Son, and Spirit, interdependent, separate but working together in unity and harmony, supported one another to turn Father's vision into a reality. *That's* Kingdom collaboration.

God's example of interdependence starts with healthy independence. Without that, we just become co-dependent, and that leads to a big fat mess. **Healthy independence looks like people who understand their true identity in Christ. They know what they bring to the table and invite others to do the same with no thought about comparison or competition. These are individuals who create out of healthy interdependent relationships with others in community for the purpose of maximum Kingdom impact.**

Let me give you a picture of how this works. Belgian draft horses are one of the strongest horse breeds in the world. A single horse can pull 8,000 pounds. One would think then that two of them could pull twice as much. Not true. Two horses working together can actually pull 20,000–24,000 pounds (nearly 3 times as much). Now to clarify, this is an example of two horses that have never met prior. If the two horses are raised and trained together, and they learn to pull and think as one, the unified pair can actually pull 30,000–32,000 pounds, almost four times as much as a single horse. Likewise, when Kingdom-minded creatives collaborate in a unified vision, they can do exponentially more than one person can do on their own.

Let me give you another example using two people pulling together instead of horses.

Johanna and Chip Gaines are the incredibly successful and highly beloved hosts of HGTV's hit show, *Fixer Upper*. From watching the series, you'd never know that Johanna professes to be a wallflower who would rather live in a safety bubble than take risks. In an interview on *White Chair Film - I Am Second®* (Oct 18, 2016), Johanna said, "If I didn't have Chip in my life I'd still be dreaming in my head. I wouldn't be acting it out; living it out. He pushed me. He pushed me out of my comfort zone. I don't want to be in the box anymore... I was created for a reason and I need to let whatever God has created me for to be known. "

Chip is not only Johanna's husband; he's someone who sees the heights of her potential and pulls her up into it. At Chip's request, Joanna agreed to have their home renovation business become a reality show for HGTV, and the rest is history. This one-time wallflower and her handy, extroverted husband married their different strengths and abilities to produce five successful seasons aired to millions of fans. They also launched numerous local businesses and a home product line in stores around the world. Could either one have achieved this level of success without the other? I think not.

Are they impacting the world for Jesus? I believe they are. They use their platform to model family values and a commitment to God. They raise children (lots of them) in the public eye, have booming businesses, work together, love each other and their family, serve their community, honor God with their lives, and have great fun and loads of laughter while doing it. They don't hide the fact that they're Christians and, judging by their popularity, their secular audience doesn't seem offended by it. Chip and Johanna are the real deal on camera and off

(I know because they stayed at my brother's vacation rental and were a delight).

I understand we're not all called to such grandiose assignments. Many of us are just starting out, dipping our little pinky toe in the water. We can't even imagine what it would be like to use our creative expression to reach millions of people around the world. That's A.O.K. God isn't calling us to be clones of Michael Gracey, Chip, or Johanna Gaines. He's calling us to fulfill the plans He has specifically for us. Thankfully, we don't have to do it alone. He is our number one collaborator, and He will guide us to the others.

Iron sharpens iron:

- Think about how many ways you collaborate with others knowingly and unknowingly: brainstorming, dreaming together, encouraging, praying, and supporting.
- In what ways would it be helpful for you to collaborate with someone on a project you're working on?
- Are there people in your community, your sphere of influence that can lend their strength to your vision?
- Make a list and then invite these individuals to pray about joining you. Be sure to share your vision with them. (Write it down make it plain - Habakkuk 2:2)

Chapter 23
Your Why, Who, & What

Let's start with a few questions:

- What is your personal life mission?
- Who is the demographic in your people group?
- What is the assignment God is highlighting to you in this season?

The first answers your "why" question. Why am I here, Lord? Your personal life mission stems from your unique identity—how you're wired—and the specific plan God has for your life. It is your calling. The second question answers your "who." Who am I called to serve, Lord, with the gifts and abilities you've given me. And the last question answers your "what." God, what do you want me to do in this season? You will need to check in from time to time with God to respond to the shifts in your assignment. Though your calling does not change, the way you carry it out may shift in various seasons of your journey.

Let's work through this together, shall we?

WHY

Our mission is our *why*. It's the reason we're here. Your mission expresses who you are as a person; defines your purpose. It includes your values, your dreams, and your passions. It should be short, just a couple of sentences or so, something you can quickly recall. Your mission statement helps you keep on track. It guides you and keeps you focused on your goals.

WHO

As Christians we are called to reach the lost—those who don't know Jesus. Additionally, there is a population that God designed you to reach. If you don't know exactly who that is, think about what makes you cry, what breaks your heart, what stirs you up to righteous anger. More than likely, it will be associated with a particular group of people. God may also call you to more than one demographic. For me, I am passionate about seeing women realize their potential, achieve their breakthroughs, and walk in greater measures of their design. I feel the same about creatives. Though there are a number of other people groups that I have a heart for, these are the primary ones that God has called me to focus on—women, creatives, and the lost. I know this because my heart burns for them.

WHAT

Your assignment is what you will do in any given season to reach the people group(s) that God has given you a burden for in the specific way that He designed you to do. Presently, God is calling me to write this book for you. It wasn't part of what He called me to do last year, but He put it on my heart in March of 2020. There are other things I'm doing now that are completely different than what God had me doing before. Everything He calls me to do surrounds my people groups and aligns with my mission. Sometimes, I'm surprised by the shifting, especially when He asks me to lay something down in order to pick up the new thing. But in all ways, I know He is being strategic and knows the big picture.

As you take the time to clarify your mission, people group, and assignment, your personal GPS will be set on the correct course heading in the right direction.

Why? What? Who? Write it down:

- What is my personal life mission—why am I here?
- Who is in my people group?
- What is the assignment God is highlighting to me in this season?

she moves
she knows
she goes
   forward
upward
     onward
to the place
where the space
in between
holds unseen
discoveries
and glimpses of mysteries
   an otherworldly dimension
     the tension between realms

Chapter 24
Show & Tell

Each one of us has a story to tell that the whole earth is groaning to hear. It's a story of sacrificial love—a daring rescue from the pit of hell through twists and turns to a promised ending of eternal happiness. It is our story.

Jesus Christ redeemed each of us from destruction. Where would we be without Him? Sometimes I think about this, and it brings me to tears. It's very possible that I wouldn't be alive. I know for sure that my life would be nothing like it is today. If I had continued down the path I was on, it wouldn't have been pretty. I can easily picture myself never getting out of bed except maybe to down some tequila and pop a few happy pills. I know for sure that hopelessness would have marked my existence.

What is your story?

How did God redeem you?

What is your testimony of His goodness in your life?

Share it.

Show it.

Tell it.

Press it into the fabric of your creative expression, whatever that might be.

"They triumphed over him by the blood of the Lamb and by the word of their testimony..."

— Revelation 12:11 (NIV)

Others need to hear the testimony of Jesus in your life so they will have hope for the testimony of Jesus in theirs. The word testimony literally means do it again.

Whether you write it, speak it, dance it, bake it, make it, whatever it looks like; be sure to share it. Your story matters because your story is God's story lived out through you!

Show & Tell:

- Recall your testimony and write it down.
- Consider ways of sharing your story in 2-3 minutes; the amount of time you might have to chat with a stranger on the street or in the store.
- Consider how you would share your story with a small group or if you were the main speaker at a conference.
- Think through how you would share your story with a secular audience.
- Get to know your story inside and out, so you are able to share it comfortably with anyone and in any situation.

Outside The Lines

(My testimony via original spoken word)

When I was young I was taught to color inside the lines. My teacher said, "This is what the best students do." And so I did too, for a while that is. But eventually, I found my greens and my blues slipping through the bars inciting a riot as the reds followed in pursuit of the oranges that giggled their way through without anyone noticing. And then all anarchy would ensue as the hues mixed and mingled, and partied hardy beyond the confines of the lines, out into the freedom of the glorious white space. Which, admittedly, was the very place I loved to be.

Oh, the endless possibilities! The adventure that awaited in the blank and pristine space where I could design my own rhyme, color my own world, dance to my own beat and be completely me, which I thought at the time, was a very good thing to be.

Now, it wasn't that I wanted to buck the system or rebel against the rails that had been erected to keep me in line, figuratively and literally. I just wanted to explore the more that I knew would be there outside the confines of those lines. I wanted a fabulous, full-spectrum color wheel—The real deal ya know, no ho-hum monochrome for me. Oh no. My life was going to be a technicolor fairytale full of fantastic adventures. Venturing outside the expected, I was going to dance with princes amid golden swirls of flickering candlelight under a canopy of stars—The start of a story that would surely end in happily ever after.

But after a while I grew older and increasingly bolder. I stepped further outside the lines, beyond the border of the white space into a whole other dimension. This new place piqued my curiosity with more possibilities for me to explore. But I found myself walking through doors that I shouldn't have walked through. Reaching for a love that was always just beyond reach. I found my freedom was misleading. It led me into forbidden territory that summoned me with a sly come hither glance, "Come on baby, you know you want to." And maybe I did want to, but that was really no reason to lose all reason.

If I had reasoned, I would have seen that I could have said no. I could have stayed safe. I could have prevented the pitfalls and all the unnecessary pain. But I didn't. And so before I knew it, I was urged forward by forces quite forceful but not at all for me (though they pretended to be).

Injustice and pain beat me again and again, pummeling my thinking and with heart sinking I drank in the liquid grays of endless cloudy days and succumbed to the ways of the dark forces at work.

And everything changed.

The lines that I first thought to confine became my hideout, my sanctuary, blocking out the world around me. The rails that I had long ago sought to destroy became the bars of my self imposed prison—Positioned perfectly to keep me from having to explain, or pretend, or comprehend anything outside the safety of those bars that barred the outside world from getting in and me from getting out.

I taught myself to stay confined within the lines where it was safe and sure and I wouldn't have to endure scrutiny. No. No one would see the part of me that I didn't want to be seen. I hid away the shades of gray and black, the backlash of a life stuck in the ashes. I became a Cinderella of sorts living in the cage of my circumstances—A dance with too many princes that all ended in destruction. For I had descended a grand staircase that spiraled downward into a pit with no glass slipper to fit and fix that which was broken in my heart.

Torn apart by wrong choices and half-baked lies I surmised that it really was my undoing this choosing to believe that life could be a technicolor freedom trail with a happily ever after ending.

NO! Finally comprehending. Freedom isn't free at all. It's pretty on the outside, ugly on the inside, a rude, crude, bait and switch plan that led me straight into the valley of the damned. I couldn't think my way out, drink my way out, play my way out, pay my way out. I couldn't talk my way out, or walk my way out. Most of all, I couldn't find my way out.

GOD! WHAT THE HELL IS ALL THIS ABOUT?

Where are You? Were You there? Did You care? Or were You thinking, "Well, young lady, you've made your bed (many times over) now just go lie in it!"

You know God, I don't think You give a rip about what I've gone through, because if You really knew and You didn't do anything to stop it then maybe You aren't so powerful.

After all, I heard, once upon a time, there was a God who loved me and died to set me free. And yet here I am imprisoned behind these bars barring any escape from the fate that I found and the endless pain that I'm bound to. This is my reality. Not a fairy tale or fantasy. It's what it is. A colorless existence, with you at a distance, and me amid the steel gray bars of my own making.

GOD! YOURS FOR THE TAKING! IF YOU WANT ME, COME AND GET ME!

Yeah, I'm talking to You God! Do you hear me? If You're real then show me—show me what You can do. Prove to me what they say is true. I have no one else. No plan B. There's just me and this massive chip on my shoulder, shouldering the weight of the world, the hate of this world. I'm tired, and pissed off. I'm bitter and maybe better off just believing in nothing and no one because then I won't get hurt. It's not worth it. I'm not worth it. Just strike me down now, God, and get this over with. I'm sure I deserve it.

Silence.

Heart beating. Thoughts retreating.

And then, a still small voice breaks in. It's in my mind, but it can't possibly be mine because it's saying things I'd never say and never think. And yet I drink it in because it's soothing to my soul and it starts to fill a hole that has been part of my heart for so long I can't remember. This voice is a stranger, yet somewhat familiar and for some strange reason, I'm not afraid of it. I turn my ear towards it. Lean into it. Press into it, I want to wrap myself in it like a blanket. It soothes me and moves me in ways I can't completely comprehend. It washes over me with liquid love, all the colors of the rainbow calling me out of my trappings—trading beauty for ashes.

Mysterious, curious, transcendent, resplendent. A vision plays out before my eyes as the Voice shows me my history and the mystery is made clear to me. Revealing that He had always been there even though I didn't see or refused to believe.

But I could see it now.

Then we traveled back even further before the foundations, before the generations and He showed how carefully, thoughtfully, he crafted me, created me to be like no other. He smiled when He talked about my penchant for color, my passion for more, my heart's desire to explore. He said, "You thought that was all you, but in fact, it was all Me. You see, those traits didn't originate in your mind, they originated in Mine. All of it was by intentional design. I was the one who created you to color outside the lines. In fact, I created the colors and I created the lines. I even created the white space that very place you loved to be outside those lines. And then, I gave you the choice, which was always yours to make, never mine.

He said, "You love freedom and so do I. That's why I gave you the freedom to make your own choices. But the voices you chose to listen to, the ones that misguided you, they were not My voice, nor would they have been My choice. But it's not just you, He said. This is true of all people. The consequence of which is great suffering upon the earth. And for what it's worth, I do see it, I did know it, and I did do something about it. I didn't turn a deaf ear or a blind eye. I gave you the one that they crucified—My very own son—The one you ignored, but He didn't ignore you. He went to the cross with your name on his lips. Sacrificed his life so you could live. He took the weight of the world, the hate of the world, it's ugliness and sin and He rose again so you could win. This is the truth. It's your choice to believe. But if you do, it will set you free.

And the Voice continued, "You see, He said, I had a plan all along because I knew this would happen. But I love you all way too much to leave you trapped in the sin you created, so I created a way out. It's not about guilt or condemnation, it's about love and redemption. You see, it's for freedom that my Son set you free. So stand firm, then, don't be burdened again by the chains of slavery. Let me show you how, let me help you out. The choices, they'll still be yours to make, but if you take the time to seek Me out; if you want to ask Me about what to do, I'll show you. I won't steer you wrong. I won't let you fail and I will never bail on you, I promise.

And He ended with this, he said, "Today is a brand new day. All the old stuff has passed away. See, my child, I'm giving you new colors.

Well, I wasn't sure if I understood it completely, but I knew there was nowhere else that I wanted to be but wrapped up in the unconditional love that beckoned me. And so I made the choice to take Him at his word and accept the truth that I believed would set me free. In that moment, I gave Him my heart and in return He gave me a brand new start.

And everything changed.

Those years of being voiceless with limited lackluster choices turned into an adventure better than any fairytale—beyond imagination—exceeding all my expectations. No longer defined or confined by the lines, I picked up my personal palette and this time I chose to paint with Him. And we set out on a path albeit unknown, but sure, because He gave me rainbow colored promises to explore.

I began to color again, outside the lines, dazzling, multi-dimensional, magnificent hues. And before I knew it, my greens and my blues slipped through the bars and incited a riot as the reds followed in pursuit of the oranges that giggled their way through without anyone noticing. And then a celebration ensued as the hues mixed and mingled and partied hardy beyond the confines of the lines and out into the freedom of the glorious white space—which, as you know, is the very place I love to be.

Oh, the endless possibilities! The adventure that awaits in the blank and pristine space where I can discover my own rhyme; uncover all the colors of my own world; dance to the beautiful beat of my own heart. And be completely me, in the freedom of all I was created to be. Hand-in-hand my Lord and me—

my happily ever after.

Section 4

Boots On The Ground

Chapter 25
Hide and Seek

ONCE YOU BEGIN your journey as a Christian creative, fulfilling the call of God on your life, you will be amazed at the power of God to work through your creativity and be humbled by His choice to use you. It's altogether thrilling and weighty and undeniably priceless.

But...

At some point or another, most, if not all of us, on this creative journey will find our counterparts basking in the limelight while we're hidden under some sort of Harry Potter-ish Cloak of Invisibility.

Imagine this: you're standing smack dab in the middle of a crowded room, a frozen smile plastered on your innocent face. You scan the room, eyes darting back and forth as you silently pray to God for someone to meet your pleading gaze. Suddenly, from across the room, someone looks in your direction. Yes! You hear the hallelujah chorus singing in your head, and you silently thank the good Lord for answering your request. Smiling back, you start walking in their direction only to discover that the person is not looking at you. They're looking at the person behind you. *Gah*! So you casually keep walking as if you're on a mission. You shift your gaze ever so slightly to the right and pretend you were smiling at someone else the whole time. One more nervous sweep of the room, and you're painfully aware that no one even noticed because no one is looking at you. You're invisible.

Some of us don't have to imagine this scene. We've lived it. And those of us who haven't yet experienced this may have that pleasure one day.

Often, we jump to the conclusion, "This must be the enemy. I'm under attack!" We give in to frustration and self-pity. We pray and wait. And wait some more. And there we sit in the middle of our disappointment, wondering why God isn't showing up to reveal His gloriousness through us like He's doing with everyone else.

But is it really an attack of the enemy? Or might it be a strategic move on the part of our sovereign Lord?

God's timing is perfect, even though it doesn't always feel that way to our sensitive egos.

Our part is to remain ready in season and out. Preparation is key. David prepared to be King while hiding in a cave. It was there that David learned how to depend on God. His faith level increased; his character was elevated; his leadership skills were honed. David's time in the cave was not wasted—it was strategic. He went into this cold dark tunnel of a cave distressed, discontented, and in debt. He came out ready to fulfill His royal role.

God sets the appointed time. If you're hidden, seek the Lord. Prepare your heart. Practice your skills, brush up on your craft, search out inspiration, continue to create. This is the perfect time to press into your faith and spend more time getting to know the One who created you to create.

God sees you. Trust that He has a brilliant strategy and in His perfect timing He will remove the Cloak of Invisibility and bring you out of the cave to continue the path to your destiny.

Creating in the Unseen:

- Write down some things you can do to encourage yourself in this hidden time and then do them.
- Check out at least one YouTube tutorial and learn a new craft or a new approach to your creative expression.
- Consider how you might lend your strength to someone who is on the front lines.
- Don't hibernate. Stay connected to your community for encouragement and support.

Chapter 26
Permission Granted

SOME OF YOU reading this book will feel a strong tug on your heart to leave the ninety-nine and go after the one. This is because you're called to be in the world (not of it) to create for mainstream secular audiences. You have ideas that take you to the edge of the edge and wonder if they're appropriate. You think maybe you're not being "Christian" enough, and your Christian community confirms this. They assume you've jumped over the edge and are swimming in the same cesspool as the rest of the ungodly world.

If you feel a burden to reach people outside the church in a way that doesn't look *church-ish*, God is calling you as a missionary to those living in great darkness; those who are not necessarily attracted to Christians or Christianity. You are God's secret weapon in these areas to reach the ones He loves. You will break through walls of hard-heartedness with creative expressions that bypass the head and go straight to the heart. And yes, it's not going to look like "normal" Christianity, but if God is in it, you can bet it will be Supernatural.

My husband grew up playing *Dungeons & Dragons (D&D)*. Though there are many who have used this role-playing game to explore dark paths, Brae and his friends quite simply enjoyed the art of creating stories within the game. Years later, after Brae had given his life to Jesus, he felt a stirring to write a book using some of his characters from

D&D. He was concerned about what the church would say, especially in light of *D&D*'s reputation for creating an atmosphere of darkness. He prayed about it and felt God say, "Don't be afraid to go into the dark places. Reveal my light." And that's what Brae did in his first book, *The Orb of Truth,* and the two books that followed in his *Horn King Series*; *The Dragon God* and *The Vampire King*. He is reaching gamers and epic fantasy action lovers through tales of good vs. evil. These are not squeaky clean stories—they have great battles, blood, gore, and a wee bit of "language." Brae did not write these books for those who are saved. He wrote them for those who are lost. He was faithful to respond to the Lord's leading. And because of this, God uses these novels to stir hearts toward Himself.

As I write this, Brae is working on a horror-thriller novel, *The Embalmer*, that is likely to offend a whole lot of Christians. The language itself will curl your teeth! But he's not writing this book for Christians; he's writing for those who don't know Jesus. God called him to leave the ninety-nine and go after the one.And he's going with guts and gusto. In the years that Brae has been writing, he's proved himself obedient to God's calling. He was responsible with smaller things and God is giving him greater things. To be clear, these particular *greater* things mean a greater risk for failure, losing Christian friends, and being thought heretical by many in the body of Christ. But there is also a greater opportunity for reward. His prayer is that secular audiences will be drawn to read the book and question their beliefs and that doors would open for him to speak to secular groups about his book. As an author speaking about his writing process, he would be able to share the gospel openly as part of his journey.

The greatest reward is an individual opening their heart to the Lord. If this comes as a result of a bloody horror novel with cuss words that would silence a sailor, then so be it. Our ways most certainly are not God's ways.

If you're called to the front lines of reaching the secular market through your creative expression (and not everyone is), then lean closely into the leading of the Lord. Let Him prepare you for the assignment. No soldier goes to the front lines without proper combat training.

Practice your weapons of warfare. Pray, abide in Him, immerse yourself in the Word, follow the leading of the Holy Spirit. Grow. Mature. Wield your weapon of breakthrough. Set your compass to True North and go for it. Permission granted!

Missionary Mindset:

- Is God calling me to leave the ninety-nine and go after the one? If yes, then answer the following questions:
- What does this assignment look like for me?
- Am I willing to sacrifice and take the risk?
- What are some of the risks and sacrifices?
- What do I need to let go of in order to move forward?
- What am I willing to do to prepare for this battle?
- Journal your responses.

Chapter 27
Stranger Than Fiction

NUMBERS 21 SHARES a story about the Israelites who are mad at God and Moses and what happens as a result. Grumbling about their sorry lot in life, they cry out, *"Why have you brought us up out of Egypt to die in the wilderness? There is no bread! There is no water! And we detest this miserable food!"* (v 5). Oy Vey!

The Israelites lost their faith, discarded any sense of gratitude, and abandoned all hope. To put it plainly, they became miserable, gossipy, cranky, back-stabbing, ingrates. (Don't judge them too harshly, though. We've all been there.)

In verse 6, we see that God sent venomous snakes, and many of the Israelites died. At that point they must have thought, *better to be miserable than dead*, so they admitted their rottenness and pleaded with Moses to ask God to take the snakes away.

Take note of what God did...

"The Lord said to Moses, 'Make a snake and put it up on a pole; anyone who is bitten can look at it and live.' So Moses made a bronze snake and put it up on a pole. Then when anyone was bitten by a snake and looked at the bronze snake, they lived." (v. 8-9)

People were completely healed by looking at a sculpture—a piece of art! Folks, you can't make this stuff up. It's in the Bible! And because it's in God's Word and God is the same yesterday, today, and forever, people can actually be healed by looking at a sculpture today...or a dance, or a film, or a painting. You get the picture. God heals through creative expression.

In 1 Samuel 16, David is called into the service of Saul, who was being tormented by evil spirits. In this case, God used another creative expression to bring healing.

"Whenever the spirit from God came on Saul, David would take up his lyre and play. Then relief would come to Saul; he would feel better, and the evil spirit would leave him." (v. 23)

This story may be stranger than fiction, but it's true nonetheless.

God called both Moses and David to create in a specific place and time for a specific purpose. They answered the call and fulfilled their respective assignments. God is calling us to do the same. His Word provides the foundation and the precedent. We can be assured that we, too, will experience God's power when we answer His call to create with Him for His purposes.

What other creative expressions can God work through? More appropriately, "Is there any creative expression that God cannot work through?"

"With people this is impossible, but with God all things are possible."
— Matthew 19:26 (NASB)

Let's feast on God's creative power in our next chapter.

the exotic chaotic
cadence of creativity
calls us to create
without caution
diving into the deep
where the
    mysteries lie
      unawakened
by unimagination
there for the taking
by those who are waking
to take the prize
    a glimpse of Your eyes
a wink and a promise

Chapter 28
Testimonies

'VE HEARD IT said that Kathryn Kuhlman took all her testimonies and imagined them like roses. She'd breathe in the fragrance and lift them to the Lord, "These are all for you."

All the testimonies I've already shared and the ones I'm about to are for the glory of the Lord. Though myself and others here have partnered with Him, the reality is that they're all from Him, through Him, and for Him. And not to tout ourselves, but to Him be the glory. (Romans 11:36)

The following testimonies are more examples of God's glorious nature and Supernatural creativity. My prayer is that they will inspire you in your creative journey with Papa God. Remember Revelation 19:10, "*The testimony of Jesus is the Spirit of prophecy.*" And the word testimony means *do it again.* So grab these testimonies for yourself and prophesy, "You did it with them, do it with me. Do it again, Daddy!"

"I was leading a class called Kingdom Create, and I encouraged the attendees to wait on the Lord to receive a prophetic picture to give to someone else. While we were doing this, we also were interceding for a woman in our community that had pain in her back and migraines. So while the students began drawing, painting, digital 'arting' (lol) the pictures the Lord had shown them, I did this quick sketch for the woman we had been praying for. I saw the Lord placing feathers along her spine, creating a healing miracle. When I was finished, I took a picture and sent it to her. I never heard back from her, but now I carried this picture on my phone.

Two months later, I attended a conference at Bethel in Redding, California called the School of Creativity. During one of the sessions, they asked people to raise their hands if they needed to be healed. They encouraged us to use our creativity to minister. There was a woman next to me who had raised her hand. Instantly I thought of the little sketch I had done. I asked her what she needed healing for, and she said she had chronic back pain that had been plaguing her for years. *What a coincidence*, I thought. So I showed her the picture I had drawn that was on my phone. I laid hands on her while she looked at the drawing, and she looked at me surprised and said she had no more back pain. She started moving and dancing around to test it out and said she could not even move like that before.

I also had extreme back pain, so much so that I had to be careful how I moved and walked so as to not throw it out. I used to be a ballerina, so not being able to move grieved me. Seeing that the woman had been healed, I said to the Lord, 'If she can be healed, so can I.' I heard the Lord beckon me to dance. Instantly, I was afraid because dancing was an absolute no-no if I didn't want to end up flat on my back. I wasn't brave enough, but at the next session, I heard him again encourage me to dance. At that point, I thought, *What do I have to lose?* I went to the back of the room and slowly started to move. Before I knew it, I was fully alive, dancing and twirling. No back pain came. I wanted to have faith I was healed but thought, *Let's see how I feel in the morning before I declare I am healed.* Sure enough, the next morning, I was still well and had been healed through my obedience to dance. That same morning, I saw the woman walking by, and she smiled at me and shouted, 'Hey! I'm healed!' We both jumped up and down and did a happy dance. She thanked me for showing her the drawing. She felt it was when she looked at it that the Lord released her healing."

Angela Hughes
imaginenowministries@gmail.com

"I was painting live at an outdoor event and stepped away for a break. Upon returning, a young woman was standing in front of my painting, weeping. I didn't want to interrupt and waited about 10 minutes before approaching her and asking if she was okay. She turned and said, 'That's me.' I asked her what she was seeing in the painting because, at that point, the piece was somewhat abstract. She said, 'It's a person being completely transformed; becoming who God created her to be…makes me cry because that's exactly where I am in life. In my darkest moments, when I feel completely hopeless, broken, without peace, and filled with turmoil, that's where He meets me.' She went on to explain my painting and put it into words more eloquently than I was able to express: 'God is meeting her in her surrender. He's pulling off each layer the world has put on her and revealing her in the most beautiful way. The colors are coming back to her.'

This young woman purchased the original later on due to the deep healing which occurred. In her words, 'I would LOVE the original…

for whatever reason I feel like He's calling me for the original. To see the paint strokes. To feel the textures. To really experience the beauty and understand the work it takes to make the beauty He has created me to be...Thinking about how far He's taken me in just 4 short months—He is so good. When we let Him in, He really brings so much light, joy, love, EVERYTHING good into our lives. It's not easy nor pain-free, but surrendering is the best decision I've ever made.' She continues to bloom as her beautiful colors are revealed for all the world to see and marvel."

"In another testimony, I was with a team in Germany, ministering to refugees from Afghanistan, Iran, Pakistan, and Syria. I asked God what to paint, and I heard: 'paint a portrait of Me.' I was shaking in my boots. This seemed impossible as:

1. I had never seen His face
2. I didn't have my normal plan and sketch prepared
3. I didn't have my normal materials. I typically use oil paints with an easel. I only had some pastels with me, no easel, so I grabbed a music stand.

Buoyed by prayer from faithful friends, I attempted to capture the essence of my Savior's likeness. As I was finishing, three refugees stood behind me. One was crying profusely, and the others had tears accompanied by smiles. I tried to ask what was going on, but the language barrier was there. I found a translator, and the weeping refugee shared, 'Now I know this Jesus because I've seen Him.' His friends were rejoicing with him as the young man accepted Jesus as his savior.'"

Mary Jordan Crawford
Mearced Art Creations
https://www.mearcedart.com

"It had been a glorious weekend of celebration in God's Presence at the worship event, David's Tent, at Del Mar Fairgrounds. Newer to exploring artistic expression through painting, I had attempted to paint a beautiful image I had envisioned in the midst of deep worship. It was of my abiding place IN Christ, at rest in a hammock in the center of His heart.

After the event, as my friend and I were pulling into our driveway,

I had a series of frightening symptoms: severe vertigo, tingling mouth and hands, and slurred speech. To my surprise, as I heard myself taking authority over the symptoms and praying in garbled, rather unintelligible speech, the symptoms subsided, and I felt fine. After a call to my doctor and a trip to the local hospital emergency room, I discovered that the source of the symptoms was not a blocked blood vessel, which leads to stroke, but a nearly closed aortic valve. What had been diagnosed as 'mild stenosis' of the valve a few years back (and still was considered 'mild' the previous year at my check-up) had rapidly advanced to critical within an unexpectedly short time. As the admitting doctor put it, "a normal aortic valve opens close to the diameter of a quarter; yours is a pinhole!"

The next few weeks were a whirlwind of activity: diagnostic tests, a non-emergency ambulance transfer to the highly-rated UCSD cardiac facility, more tests, and meetings with 3 different surgical teams. I then needed to make the weighty decision on which of several surgical approaches to take for the repair. Being constantly monitored and unable to safely go home, I was hospitalized for two weeks as they sought to get me into the busy schedule. I remained for another week after having the open-heart surgery.

The outpouring of love and prayer from friends and family near and far was tangible (and overwhelming at times). The peace, comfort, and even joy I was carried in, by God and through the prayers of many, was astonishing and totally unexplainable to the natural mind. I encountered and experienced the 'peace that *passes_understanding*' that Jesus gifted His followers with. I had no fear. I even had several uproariously fun times with visitors in those weeks!

But here is the incredible reality of God's faithfulness—I *lived* the very image I had painted at the worship event before any of this had even happened. My God had gone before me, faithfully preparing the way, faithfully preparing ME, and faithfully giving me the very best the medical field had to offer. The painting is my 'stone of remembrance.' I kept it by my hospital bedside the whole time, and it is still speaking and empowering my abiding place every day."

Susan Morningstar

"Is it okay to write about Vampires during worship?

I had published two books in my young adult epic fantasy series and was working feverishly on completing the third called The Vampire King. I had discovered that creativity flowed extremely powerful during times of worship. It was at a worship event that I received the epic ending of my first book, The Orb of Truth. And it was during many church worship services that I received major downloads of plots, characters, and interesting twists and turns for my second novel. I took notice of this and actually pursued writing at many events in the San Diego region. At the time, worship was exploding all across our county, with multiple worship leaders coming together to provide 24- to 72-hour worship events.

With my third book, I decided to write during every worship event, including times at church. I set up a table in the back of the room, brought my laptop, and wrote for the forty-five minute (minimum) worship set at our church, The Awakening, in Carlsbad, California. Many people were wondering what I was doing, and I told them I was worshiping God through my writing. Sometimes I would look up to heaven and think, *God, this is crazy. I'm sitting here during worship writing about vampires.* But each time I would get the sense that God was smiling at me, enjoying every minute of it. The Vampire King was published in August of 2015.

The following year, God led me to launch Kingdom Writers Association to help equip, empower, and encourage Christian writers to write for God. At one of our monthly gatherings, a young man at the age of around 18 asked to speak to me privately. We stepped outside, and he began to tell me how much he enjoyed my epic fantasy series. It was when he got to talking about *The Vampire King* specifically that he started to get emotional. Through tears, he expressed how much one of the characters spoke to him. He remarked about how this character loved so deeply that he would do anything for the love of his life, so much so that he sacrificed his own and became a vampire. This made a deep impression on this young man.

One of the questions that I had when writing *The Vampire King* was, 'Can a vampire be saved?' This was the premise I explored through this particular book. The young man who pulled me aside that day was wrecked by the love expressed by an 'unlikely' character in the book and compared it to the love of Jesus. He shared, 'This ministered to my heart, and I want to thank you.'

Wow, that ministered to me! But it also showcased the power of God and how our writing, even a fantasy book written during worship and involving a vampire, can be used by Him."

Brae Wyckoff, Director of Kingdom Writers Association
https://www.KingdomWritersAssociation.com
https://www.BraeWyckoff.com

"About nine years ago, God put on my heart to create jewelry and sell it. Our church at the time held many conferences, and people were encouraged to set up a table with their creative items, whatever they may be.

I was highly involved in Graham Cooke's ministry when he was part of this church and had learned about and operated extensively in the prophetic thanks to Graham. When I asked God about the jewelry—which. by the way, I had never made before, He told me He would give me the idea for each piece and then give me a prophetic word to go with each item.

It was such an exciting time and a huge learning curve for me, but I was obedient. I prayed over each necklace and blessed it, hoping it would touch someone. For me, it wasn't about the money but has been and always will be about the act of obedience. As Graham Cooke's conference drew closer, I had made about a dozen necklaces and attached a prophetic word in writing to each. I left my jewelry at the table with the women who were manning it and went to participate in the conference. I never actually believed my jewelry was good enough to sell, and at the price a friend helped me to decide upon. I didn't value it enough to think someone else would, but boy was I soon to learn otherwise.

After the conference was over and I hesitantly walked up to the table. Fearing that not one piece of my jewelry would have sold, I discovered that every single necklace was purchased. The women manning the table had many stories of how each person who purchased one of my necklaces had a story. Not only the piece of jewelry spoke to them, but the prophetic words were spot on, delivering them, healing them, setting them free right on the spot! There were a couple of women who found me as I was pointed out by the women selling my necklaces. They each had bought necklaces and were in tears at how good God was to speak into right where their need was. There was confirmation and affirmation for them and for me too. They were beyond thankful and loved the jewelry, sharing that it will always remind them of the time God spoke powerfully to them in an unexpected way.

Needless to say, I was excited and so humbled by it. I thought back on how I didn't know anything about jewelry making, and once I learned, my thoughts were, *who would want to buy this*? Typical self doubts coming from the enemy of our soul. Responding to God's call and making those necklaces grew me in trusting to hear the voice of

God. My reliance and obedience to Him went to new levels as well as experiencing the reality that God can speak through anything."

Robby Little

"This is my favorite story of one of the first prophetic cakes I ever made. I had a dear friend order a cake for a birthday celebration for someone she knew. I had never met this lady before, so I knew nothing about her. As I created this cake for her, I felt God speaking to me and showing me specific things that he wanted to minister to her and encourage her in. With every prophetic cake I do, I always type up the word and scriptures so that the person can read them as they are eating their cake. I absolutely love God's creativity with this idea because they are getting to consume the prophetic word as it is shared. They literally get to 'TASTE and see that the Lord is good!' (Psalm 34:8).

This celebration was one of the few times I got to personally read the word over them. When I was finished, she was so touched. Everything that was shared was timely and exactly what she needed to hear. In that moment, God brought her a renewed joy and encouragement for her future. The other ladies in the room were not Christians and never experienced anything like that before. After I had left, they asked if I was 'psychic.' My friend then got the opportunity to share with them that I am a Christian and that God speaks to me through my creativity to show his love to the person receiving it. In that moment. not only did God minister to the person receiving the cake, but He also set the atmosphere for everyone else attending the birthday celebration to be ministered to as well!

"In another testimony, There was an evening a couple years ago I had one of my dear friends over. We were having a wonderful girl's night, and towards the end of our time together, I offered her a cookie. Before she ate it, I prayed for God's anointing, love, and healing to be released through every bite she ate and for Him to release whatever He wanted to do in her life. As soon as she took the first bite,

God immediately pulled her into a full encounter with him. In that encounter, she felt the love of God wash over her and touch her heart in a deep and profound way (There had been a lot of heart trauma and pain she had experienced over the past several years). In that moment, God began healing her heart from all of those wounds. That encounter lasted for about 30 minutes to an hour. When He was finished ministering to her, her demeanor had completely changed. All of the weight, burden, and sadness had fallen away and, in exchange, there was a renewed hope, joy, freedom."

Brittany Zaninovich
Taste and Sea Cakery
https://www.tasteandseacakery.com/

"In May of 2017, I had a constant cough for about a month that I just could not seem to shake. As a working mom of two young children, I pushed through and kept things rolling, assuming my body would eventually heal, and I would be at full strength again. I had planned to go to Bethel School of Creativity, and I refused to miss it. I promised my husband that I would see a doctor when I returned home. My cough was so intense that a friend loaned me her inhaler to help me get through the days. While at the Bethel School of Creativity conference, God gave me a picture of my lungs, and I knew that I needed to draw them and release healing over myself. I had a couple of friends agree with me, we released my healing, and then we carried on with the weekend. When I came home, the doctor told me I had bronchitis and gave me medicine. At this point, I had not been able to sleep in a bed for several weeks. I had to sit upright and lean forward to breathe & not cough constantly. I started the medication, and a day or two later, I stopped breathing. I was intubated and spent five days in the ICU. During my time in the ICU, I knew I was already healed because God had already given it to me when He gave me the picture of my lungs, and we released my healing. He sent healing angels to me when I was in the ICU. They were assigned to bring healing on a cellular level. I knew it was going to be ok because I had a promise. Today, I am still walking in healing & health. It has been a journey of recovering my physical strength and overcoming mental & emotional obstacles, but God kept the promise He gave me through the picture of my healed lungs. I am WELL!"

Charity Williams

"Over the past year, we have all been stretched by God, but when we are obedient, we can always see His hand in the result. In this particular instance, we planned a half-day of filming an episode for our new ministry. The plan was very simple. It would be a quick drawing for a give-away, followed by a short teaching segment. We would wrap this up by Noon and be ready for a lunch date with a friend for her birthday. The drawing went just as planned, and we quickly moved onto the teaching, excited to be able to go to lunch (and dessert, of course) right afterwards.

We had ordered a new teleprompter (as I really wanted to share some very specific things and didn't want to risk forgetting any of it) and worked for some time to set it up. We tried for a couple of hours to get it to work, but we were unsuccessful. Since we always pray before beginning any filming, I knew that this situation was covered in prayer and that God was in control. It seemed like we should press in with more prayer and ask Holy Spirit what to do next. After quite some time in prayer and worship, I felt it pressed upon my spirit that we were not to film the segment as we had planned but rather give our viewers an opportunity to receive the Lord as their Savior. This is exactly what we did.

When we reached out to the winner of the drawing, she informed us that she had seen our video and watched it through to the end. She also accepted the Lord as her Savior during the prayer time. Furthermore, when my partner took the teleprompter home to try to fix it, her unsaved husband helped her to read what was on the teleprompter, which was the Word of God. We all know that His Word does not return void."

Jeanette Bradley
Radiant Pearls Ministry
https://radiantpearlsministries.com/

"I never thought I had a story in me, and definitely not a testimony for that matter. As we headed into the restaurant for dinner, I had no idea this was all about to change. One evening while celebrating the birthday of a pioneer in Christian broadcasting, my ministry partner and I were asked to write an article for a new women's magazine that was preparing to launch. We were given five days to write this article. We jumped for joy at the offer! As we left dinner that night, I questioned whether my decision was the right one. This would be the first article I would write about, well, me.

For the next two days, all I could do was think about the article, but every time I went to write it, I had nothing. And I mean nothing. My mind was blank. It just didn't seem like I had any huge, life-changing testimony to share. The night before it was due, I was determined to put something on that page. So, I prayed and went at it. The Lord began to remind me of what I had experienced, who I was, and the habits I used to have. He showed me that I am not that person anymore. He also reminded me of where I am now and what He has done in and through me. Within a few hours, it was done! I had written my testimony—the one I never thought I had.

A few short weeks later, the magazine that included my testimony was released. I could not believe that my testimony was printed in a magazine! Two weeks after the magazine was published, I was asked to give my testimony at a service. After sharing my testimony, yet again, I was overwhelmed by the responses that I received from many people who were inspired. Shortly after sharing my testimony, I was given an opportunity to write a chapter in a book called I QUIT! This book released a short time later and became a bestseller! Just two and-a-half short months after discovering I had a testimony, it was printed in a magazine, shared before a congregation, and printed in a best-selling book!

I encourage you to write that testimony that I know is in you and let God show you what He can do with your obedience."

Justina Sanchez
Radiant Pearls Ministries
https://radiantpearlsministries.com/

"As a worship leader, I have had the honor of seeing people saved, healed, and set free in services I've been a part of. I have also been encouraged by many who say they can feel the tangible presence of God whenever I sing. There is one testimony that really stands out of God moving through my song. It was Choir Sunday, and I was leading worship. Sarah was part of the choir and was singing with the background vocals for the first time. Sarah described herself as a church-goer. She was excited to serve in the church, but that was the extent of her relationship with God. There was no deep connection to Jesus or a desire for a closer walk with Him. However, God was moving powerfully in Sarah's life to reveal Himself to her.

During the service, I led 'Revelation Song,' which contains a beautiful musical interlude.

It was during this interlude that Sarah said, 'You began to preach.' I would describe it more as exhorting or leading the people into a deeper place of worship. It was then that Sarah said she felt the presence of God come over her body. She closed her eyes and saw a vision. In the vision, she saw the hands and feet of Jesus with holes and blood dripping down. Then she heard a voice say, 'Do you think I did this for nothing?' Tears began to stream down Sarah's face as she took in the sight, and thought of the sacrifice Jesus made for her. As she stood there in the presence of God, she said her tongue began to flip and flop on its own. She wasn't sure what was happening, but she didn't doubt it was God. I was so filled with awe and joy to learn that the Lord was moving so powerfully during the worship. I was able to explain to her the wonderful gift Jesus had given her as we looked at the Scriptures and how Jesus baptizes with the Holy Spirit and fire. I explained to her that she was able to use her new prayer language as often as she wanted and that she should use it all the time. I explained to her how the Holy Spirit prays through our spirit and illuminates our understanding of scripture and hearing God's voice. I showed her how the gifts of the Spirit are available for us to expand God's kingdom and transform us. It was wonderful.

There was a domino effect happening in Sarah's life and from that moment she was never the same. Sarah says she went from being 'a church fan to a Jesus follower.' There was now a hunger inside of her for more of God. She was now making time for prayer and bible reading, and as she continued to attend small group and seek God, she learned how to draw near for herself. The transformational power of God spread to the entire family, and they were also baptized in the Holy Spirit shortly after.

Sarah and her husband subsequently enrolled in school and became licensed ministers who desire to see all people know God and experience His love. As I was talking to Sarah and remembering this day, I was once again filled with such awe and wonder at how the Lord moves. Worship ministry is a powerful way to encounter God, and it is so much more than goosebumps. When we are in the presence of God, chains of bondage fall, bodies are healed, and lives are changed forever. Sarah's story inspires me to press in for more of His Spirit and to encourage our worship teams to release the Spirit of God through our song every time we get the opportunity. 'Where the Spirit of the Lord is, there is freedom.' 2 Corinthians 3:17"

DeeDee Whitley
https://www.lovemovementministries.org

Food for thought:

- Is art the finished product or the process? Journal your thoughts.
- Write down the testimony of how God is guiding you through your process.
- As you experience your own testimonies as a result of creating with God, write them down (stones of remembrance) and share them to encourage others.

Section 5
Remember

Chapter 29
Who Am I?

ALONG THE WAY, it is highly likely that we will encounter opposition and be tempted to doubt what we're doing, why we're doing it, and if we can do it right. These thoughts may even come as a surprise to us because we've already experienced overcoming and breakthrough in these areas. We may feel betrayed by our own thoughts and discouraged from moving forward. Don't be. This is all part of the journey.

When we experience disappointment, discouragement, and doubt, it will serve us well to remind ourselves about what we learned at the beginning of this book and HIS book. We are created in the image and likeness of our Master Creator—our Papa God. He has a plan for our life, and He designed us with everything we need to fulfill it. He has gifted us and called us to carry out our assignment in collaboration with His Spirit. Together with Him, we will bring Supernatural restoration and redemption through our creative expression—whatever that expression may be—because His will *will* be done on earth as it is in heaven.

When we bring to remembrance the Truth of God's Word and what He says about us, our hearts are stirred to respond accordingly. From this position, we can step boldly and confidently into that Truth and fulfill our Divine assignment.

Supernatural creativity is conceived in the heart of God and birthed out of the heart of His children, fully aligned with their identity in Christ.

This is what I know about you and what I want you to know about yourself: You are a walking-talking testimony to the faithfulness and goodness of a Master Creator who created you to live large and shine bright—to shine His light through everything you do and everything you create. You can do this not because you are perfect but because He is perfect. You are a Kingdom Creative who imagines without limitation and creates without a thought for comparison, competition, performance, perfectionism, rejection, or fear. You create because you cannot help but do so. Creativity is woven into the fiber of your being. God, Himself, was the weaver. And you believe it—even though the enemy wants you to doubt it. You believe it on your darkest days. You believe it when you're at the top of your game and at the bottom of the dogpile. You believe it when you're clearly seen and when you're hidden under that Harry Potter-ish Cloak of Invisibility. You believe it because you've tasted and seen the goodness of the Lord in the land of the living. You belong to Him, and you are fully aware that He's got you. Even in the midst of your process, He's got you. And He's never letting go.

Remembering:

- Read back through your notes from the beginning of this book.
- Meditate on what stands out to you.
- Pick one or two highlights, write them on a note card and tuck it away for later, when the doubt starts creeping in and you need reminding.
- Pull out scriptures that speak about who you are as God's child and Christ's follower. Write them down in your journal or on post-its and place them where you will see them and be reminded.

Who do you think you are?

"Know the truth and the truth will set you free."

- John 8:32

Chapter 30
Who Is He?

I N THE LAST chapter, I talked about the importance of remembering what God says about you, who you are as His child, and your identity in Christ. All of this is moot if you don't have an appropriate understanding of who God is.

Yes, we all know that God is astoundingly wonderful, but there can be a tendency to take a step back from Him when things are going good and press in with all we have when things are not. One minute we're saying, "God, I need you like crazy!" And the next minute, we're coasting through life thinking, "God, I got this." But here's the problem with that. Those who disconnect, even for a short while, will most likely wind up relying more on their own abilities than God's. Inevitably, their faith will falter with each passing disappointment and seemingly unanswered prayer. Without consistent connection, they will suffer the highs and lows of emotion like a bucking bronco rider. Try as they might to hold on for dear life, sooner rather than later, they will end up on the ground with a sore bum and a black and blue ego.

Mature creatives are those who continuously press in; consistently seek after the Lord and remind themselves of His nature and His will.

In the beginning of this book, I shared scripture and science that revealed the immensity of our God. Though we can use all kinds of words to define him: Majestic, Creator, all-powerful, ever-present, all-knowing, sovereign, provider, protector, faithful, good, and so on, He truly is beyond description. There is no end to Him. He does not fit inside our finite boxes. We will spend all eternity getting to know Him and still not uncover everything there is to discover. He's *that* big!

I encourage you to meditate on His Word daily. Get to know Him better. Abide in Him. The more you know about your Father God, the more you'll understand about yourself as His son or daughter. This is the key to walking in the fullness of your identity in Christ and producing consistent Supernatural creativity. From here, anything is possible.

Seek Him First:

- What is your favorite way to experience the awe and wonder of God?
- What can you do to remind yourself of who God is to you?
- How will you choose to commune with God today? Tomorrow? Ongoing?
- Write a poem about your relationship with God (You don't have to show it to anyone).

Chapter 31
Protein Snack

HAVE YOU EVER had one of those mornings where you thought you had more time than you did, only to find you're running fifteen minutes late, and you have no time to make yourself a decent breakfast before you hit the road? You dash out to the car in frustration, "If only I had gotten up twenty minutes earlier, I could have eaten. Ugh!" Your stomach starts to growl, and you growl back. You wonder how you'll ever last till lunch. Maybe your coworker will find you passed out on your desk from sheer starvation. Your imagination is spiraling out of control. Your mood is slipping dangerously close to the pit of despair. And then, just before you hit rock bottom, you remember that you have a whole bag of almonds in your top right desk drawer. In the back of your mind, you hear a choir of angels start to sing the hallelujah chorus, and you know you've been saved.

Thank God for protein!

That's what this chapter is all about. It's the protein snack to feed your soul when you don't have time for a full breakfast.

In this section, I've taken the highlighted points that I've written throughout this book and placed them linearly here in one chapter. At some point in your creative journey, you may need to remind your soul of what your mind already knows. You may be feeling a bit shaky and need some sustenance to tide you over. Take a bite or two, or more if you have time. Chew on these tasty little morsels and get reenergized. This isn't the whole enchilada but it's packed with protein and will sustain you till your next meal.

Bon appétit!

You carry the genetic markings of the creator of EVERYTHING. In Genesis, God is very clear about His design, so you'll be very clear about yours.

Some of us have always felt different—like we're not like everyone else. That's because we're not. There never has been nor ever will be anyone on the planet who is exactly like you. This is by intentional design—our DNA confirms it.

Only you can disqualify you from being creative. Here's the reality—if you're breathing, you're creative. Why? Because you take after your Father God.

As the redeemed of the Lord, we carry His Holy Spirit. We've always had the ability to create because we bear the image of our Papa God. Our salvation gives us access and authority to collaborate with the Holy Spirit and release more than just pretty things and good ideas. Our creative expressions are infused with the manifest power and presence of God to reveal His nature.

He placed His creative nature *in* you to reveal Himself *through* you.

God always has more for us than we can dream of. And He's given us everything we need to accomplish it. One of the biggest mistakes you or I can make is to believe that God cannot use little ol' us.

It has nothing to do with what we, as creatives, produce. It's all about what God can produce through us.

It's not about *becoming* someone new; it's about *discovering* who you were always designed to be.

We must let go of any belief that does not line up with what God says about us, or we will either paralyze ourselves into inactivity, move in a direction that is not God's best for us, or tread a weird combination of both that has us starting and stopping but never getting anywhere.

Breakthrough begins with recognizing that God is your Master Creator and what He says about you is true.

Our response to the Lord requires putting our beliefs into action, not just lip service. The Bible says that God puts His Spirit in us to "*move*" us (Ezekiel 36:27). He's waiting for us to move.

When we rely completely on God, He will never let us down. That's how it gets easier. We do it together—100% Him, 100% us—and He does all the heavy lifting.

Our calling as believers doesn't change. We are called into fellowship with God's Son, Jesus Christ—this is the first and highest calling. From this position, we can love others as ourselves and carry out the great commission (Matthew 16:19-20). The way we carry out our calling, however, differs from person to person according to their individual design and changes from season to season according to God's assignment.

We can create because He first created. We are able to do so because of what He did. We can be thankful for the gifts He has given us and acknowledge Him for them while at the same time accept our contribution. It's not about showing off but rather acknowledging our part in showing *Him* off.

The Bible says, "*whatever the man called each living creature, that was its name.*" Not only does God reveal His desire to co-labor with man, but gives credence to the fact that man has an innate God-given ability to imagine. God did not doubt Adam's imagination; He encouraged him to exercise it.

God does not coddle mindsets rooted in fear or lack—our current condition does not pose a threat to His plans. He was unfazed by Mary's situation, and He's not rattled by yours. Why? Because the power of the Holy Spirit—God Himself—will co-labor with us to manifest His decrees.

There is so much that God can do through a willing partner. He wants to author your story and perfect your faith. There is only one way to test the level of your faith—walk it out. Trust that God will do what He says He will do.

Everything that came into being started with one simple step—a move toward a goal.

I once was shy and embarrassed about displaying any part of myself or my work. Now I am bold. It's not because of *what* I carry—It's because of *WHO* I carry.

Process isn't always easy to walk through, but it is the only way to get from one place to another.

In the midst of the process is where we find out what we're made of; mine the gold within us and uncover the treasure that was always there beneath the surface waiting to be discovered. It's where God shows up in ways that you never dreamed possible and invites you to experience Him on a whole new level. It is an exhilarating adventure that begins with a single step and climbs to heights beyond your imagination.

We cannot create without "The Force" and expect to win against our evil nemesis. With God, all things are possible, and without Him, nothing is possible. Victory is in the Lord. Invite Him in for the win!

Your creative expression is directly affected, positively or negatively, by the level of connection you have with your Creator.

God, in human form, was surrounded by suffering and injustice. He felt every possible emotion. And yet, He was so connected to His Father He did not buckle nor bow to lesser worldly gods: angst, fear, shame, rejection, hopelessness, or pride. In vulnerability and humility, with all His emotions in tow, Jesus reassured and sustained Himself through intentional connection with the source of absolute truth and perfect love—His Daddy.

When we disconnect from worldly perspectives and connect to Papa God, our creative expressions will reflect His righteousness. As a result of Divine connection and collaboration, our natural abilities will take on Supernatural power. This is the life of a creative devoted to the One who calls them to create—a life lived in the flow of the Holy Spirit.

Comparison leads to disqualification by paralysis. It turns a blind eye to the fact that we were created uniquely to reveal God's heart in a way that only we can do. It denies diversity and God's plan to extend His Kingdom through each and every one of His children. It believes that God did not create you with everything you need to fulfill His plans through you. Comparison believes in a lesser god.

There is only one person we should ever compare ourselves to, and that's Jesus. Though we will never measure up, we are to become more and more Christlike. In becoming more like Jesus, we do not lose ourselves but rather become a greater version of ourselves, a fuller expression of our original design.

In the Kingdom, when our brother or sister succeeds in their God-given assignment, we celebrate their victory. There is no competition—no jealousy. We understand that our mission is the same: to glorify God through our creative expression and see Jesus get His reward. In this, a win for one is a win for the Kingdom, and a win for the Kingdom is a win for all.

Who is perfect? Jesus. That's it. The rest of us have no shot at perfection. This isn't derogatory. It's a good thing. It should remove any attempt to try.

The Father of Lies works to keep us running on a hamster wheel of futility, chasing after perfectionism as a righteous goal and a noble prize. Meanwhile, he's offside snickering at the knowledge that this race will never be won. And worse, that some of us will die trying.

Performance says you must continuously strive to be better than you are. Not from a healthy sense of personal growth and maturity, but because the familiar whip of failure might strike at any moment. Performance bears the scars of not being enough.

Our destiny is not based on our performance—it is based on our surrender.

Because our confidence is in Christ and our competence comes from God, we can rest assured that man's rejection has no bearing on us.

Fear causes us to take short breaths and live small lives. It tells us that it's okay to stay in our comfort zone. It pitches in and helps us build a safety net around ourselves. Fear whispers, "Just give up. Take the easy way out. It won't cost you anything." In reality, it will cost you everything. It will cost you your God-given destiny.

Take the opportunity to carve out space in your schedule for playtime. It doesn't matter how old we are; we are all God's kids. Explore with childlike wonder and discover there's more to you than you thought.

Jesus went off and prayed, firm in His identity as a child of God who needed time alone with His Daddy. He didn't do anything He didn't see His Father doing or say anything He didn't hear His father saying. He was perfectly childlike—completely dependent on His Papa; postured as a Son.

All creativity is birthed out of imagination; first God's, then yours.

When we create, we tap into His sanctified imagination. It is neither frivolous nor useless—it is Holy.

Imagination is not just an inconsequential by-product of our humanity. It is purposed to be an essential connection with Divinity.

Who am I? Only Jesus gets to answer that question. We are defined through Him and by Him.

Identity is actualized on the front lines.

Our goal shouldn't be to get people to like us but to be the fullest manifestation of the revelation of our design.

The more you learn about God, the more you'll discover about yourself. The chrysalis of self-doubt and false identity will not be able to contain you any longer.

God's answer to a godless kingdom, in Zechariah's time and now, is His craftsmen—His creatives. We are his mighty warriors. He is calling us to the front lines to *terrify* the enemy through creative expression!

Our creative expressions, imbued with the power of the Holy Spirit, have the power to save, heal, deliver, transform, reform, and restore. Its universal language breaks down barriers, provokes thought, inspires, enlightens, and sets a table for God to come in and dine.

God's army of creatives have been given the authority to reach their communities for Christ with revelation expressed through creativity. When we collaborate with the Holy Spirit, we take His thoughts and make them visible through our creative expression, bringing the unseen into the seen to create works and innovations that are prophetic in nature.

God's prophetic voice comes in every size, shape, and color. It defies logic and deftly outmaneuvers our propensity to stuff it in the itty-bitty box of our own expectations. When we let Him put His hand on ours and create with us, our creative expressions carry His voice to their intended audience and draws them closer to His heart. In this way, everything we create with him becomes a powerful tool for outreach— to prophesy and evangelize.

Regardless of whether you think you've got it all together and are fully capable of doing what you're called to do, or you believe you aren't the least bit qualified, your starting point is the exact same—total surrender.

When we create out of relationship with our Heavenly Father, intersected with His Spirit, we submit our words and works to His direction and give Him room to move in purpose and supernatural power.

All creatives need each other. They need to be among their people; those who can encourage them to stay the course; those who inspire them to go to their next level. You may have heard it said that isolation is the devil's playground. If that's true, and I believe from experience that it is, then the opposite must also be true. Community is God's playground.

Supernatural creativity is not a one-man show. First and foremost, we collaborate with the Holy Spirit, and then God brings others to lend their strengths and support to the vision.

Healthy independence looks like people who understand their true identity in Christ. They know what they bring to the table and invite others to do the same with no thought about comparison or competition. These are individuals who create out of healthy interdependent relationships with others in community for the purpose of maximum Kingdom impact.

As you take the time to clarify your mission, people group, and assignment, your personal GPS will be set on the correct course heading in the right direction.

Others need to hear the testimony of Jesus in your life so they will have hope for the testimony of Jesus in theirs. The word testimony literally means do it again. Whether you write it, speak it, dance it, bake it, make it, whatever it looks like, be sure to share it. Your story matters because your story is God's story lived out through you!

God sets the appointed time. If you're hidden, seek the Lord. Prepare your heart. Practice your skills, brush up on your craft, search out inspiration, continue to create. This is the perfect time to press into your faith and spend more time getting to know the One who created you to create.

If you feel a burden to reach people outside the church in a way that doesn't look *church-ish*, God is calling you as a missionary to those living in great darkness; those who are not necessarily attracted to Christians or Christianity. You are God's secret weapon inthese areas to reach the ones He loves. You will break through walls of hard-heartedness with creative expressions that bypass the head and go straight to the heart. And yes, it's not going to look like "normal" Christianity, but if God is in it, you can bet it will be Supernatural.

God called both Moses and David to create in a specific place and time for a specific purpose. They answered the call and fulfilled their respective assignments. God is calling us to do the same. His Word provides the foundation and the precedent. We can be assured that we, too, will experience God's power when we answer His call to create with Him for His purposes.

When we bring to remembrance the Truth of God's Word and what He says about us, our hearts are stirred to respond accordingly. From this position, we can step boldly and confidently into that Truth and fulfill our Divine assignment.

Supernatural creativity is conceived in the heart of God and birthed out of the heart of His children, fully aligned with their identity in Christ.

Mature creatives are those who continuously press in, consistently seek after the Lord, and remind themselves of His nature and His will.

As Kingdom Creatives, we understand that if we get commended and celebrated for our work it's ok to say, "Thank you." God isn't elevated by our downplaying our role. We are pleased with the work of our hands because we create with our hands placed in His. We are pleased with the work of our mind because we have the mind of Christ. We are pleased with the work of our heart because we express a part of His heart that no one else can express. We can do nothing without Him and everything with Him. No false humility. No lack of humility. We simply do the work God gave us to do in partnership with Him.

Section 6
Released

Chapter 32
Success And Humility

THROUGHOUT THIS BOOK, we've seen what God can do through His creatives and Supernatural creativity. As we approach the conclusion, I want to address what it looks like as we begin to advance in our status as creatives. How do we walk in humility when we're getting paid a lot of money, or when we've achieved a measure of notoriety and our work is highly publicized? How do we remain humble when the very act of marketing and advertising feels boastful? Is it wrong to put yourself out there in the public eye or receive attention for your work?

Of course not. The key is to remember *who* called you and gifted you to do what you're doing and *whose* work you're promoting.

The Bible tells us that God knows our hearts. Do you love Jesus? Are you working for His fame or your own? We may think the answers are obvious. Of course, I love Jesus and want to make Him famous! But what happens when you're leaving the ninety-nine to go after the one and it's not so obvious? What happens when, like my husband, you're writing for the secular market and not overtly preaching the gospel of Jesus through your creative expression? Are you really making His name famous or hiding Him and promoting your own name? There may be those who think the latter. They may even have you second-guessing your true motives. Be at peace. God knows your heart. After all, He's the One who called you to this special assignment in the first place.

As Kingdom Creatives, we understand that if we get commended and celebrated for our work it's ok to say, "Thank you." God isn't elevated by our downplaying our role. We are pleased with the work of our hands because we create with our hands placed in His. We are pleased with the work of our mind because we have the mind of Christ. We are pleased with the work of our heart because we express a part of His heart that no one else can express. We can do nothing without Him and everything with Him. No false humility. No lack of humility. We simply do the work God gave us to do in partnership with Him.

Whatever the outcome, it is God that makes our work Supernatural and God that brings us any measure of success—no matter how great or small. Because of this, we can graciously receive any manner of fame, fortune, and accolades with great gratitude for to Him be *all* the glory!

Chapter 33
Commissioning

*But you are a chosen race, a royal priesthood, a holy
nation, a people for his own possession, that you may
proclaim the excellencies of him who called you out of
darkness into his marvelous light.*

—1 Peter 2:9

THIS IS WHO you are and what you're called to do.

I bless you to know that you are a royal priesthood chosen by
God to proclaim His excellencies.

I bless you to acknowledge and celebrate your God-given creative
expression and your creative journey from your humble beginnings on
forward.

The Lord commissions you to proclaim God in the way you were
uniquely designed to do, using your creative gifts to reveal His glory.
To create with God, for God, to reveal God.

The Lord commissions you to use your creative expression to
advance the Kingdom of God supernaturally; to bring restoration and
hope; to shift the atmosphere, and to impact the world around you for
Jesus.

The Lord commissions you to press on toward the goal to win the prize for which God has called you heavenward in Christ Jesus; to run your race boldly without fear of man or fear of failure.

The Lord commissions you to proclaim the Word of God and stand upon it no matter what! Rise to the occasion and preach when it is convenient and when it is not. Preach in the full expression of the Holy Spirit. Preach through your creative expression in the power of the Holy Spirit. Create with wisdom.

For we are living in a time where our society no longer listens and responds to the healing words of truth because they have become selfish and proud, and they listen to those with words that line up with their desires, saying just what they want to hear. They close their ears to the truth, but you carry the secret weapon to revealing the truth in a way that breaks down barriers. You carry the Gospel of Jesus in and through your creative expression. You are commissioned to plant those seeds—evangelize through your creative expression and fulfill your ministry calling.

The Lord commissions you to make the most of the time God has given you, fight the good fight, finish your full course, and keep your heart full of faith.

My prayer for you:

"For this reason, I kneel before the Father, from whom every family in heaven and on earth derives its name. I pray that out of his glorious riches he may strengthen you with power through his Spirit in your inner being, so that Christ may dwell in your hearts through faith. And I pray that you, being rooted and established in love, may have power, together with all the Lord's holy people, to grasp how wide and long and high and deep is the love of Christ, and to know this love that surpasses knowledge—that you may be filled to the measure of all the fullness of God.

Now to him who is able to do immeasurably more than all we ask or imagine, according to his power that is at work within us, to him be glory in the church and in Christ Jesus throughout all generations, for ever and ever! Amen."

— Ephesians 3:14-21 (NIV)

Afterword

Today is January 17, 2021, and I'm getting one step closer to finalizing this book and getting it into your hands. But before I send it off to the editor, I have one more thing on my mind.

A couple of days ago, I had a conversation with a friend about "spiritual things." Fully aware of my belief in Jesus Christ, she began to ask me questions about my faith, which, as you can imagine, I was only too happy to talk about. She then shared her experiences with Yoga and Reike, her longing for a deeper connection to the Divine, and her gravitation towards New Age spirituality. This launched a whole conversation about the Holy Spirit vs. other spirits, the longing that we all have in our hearts for something greater than ourselves (by design), and the choice God gives us to choose Him. Typically, I would have followed up with all the glorious benefits of choosing Christianity. But to my amazement, the Holy Spirit took me in a totally different direction.

This is what I said.

> I get it. Choosing to go the New Age route is easy. You can move in and out, feel good, do it again; don't feel good, change it up till you find something that makes you feel better. It's easy. You just go after what feels good to you. Christianity is different because Christianity requires something of you. I'm not talking about going to church. I'm talking about sacrifice, about remaining in faith and trusting God when things don't go the way you want them to. It's responding to His call and

His leading when it's uncomfortable and you don't think you can do it. It's not like you become a Christian and everything is *la-di-da* and perfect. It's work. It's sacrifice. It's commitment.

A part of me couldn't believe the words that were coming out of my mouth. I thought, *Great, I'm going to turn her completely off Christianity! Her life is hard enough, and now I'm telling her she can't just flip a switch and make it easier.*

But she can flip a switch and make it *better*.

I told her about Jesus.

And in the end, I assured her that even though it requires something, the benefits far outweigh the cost. There is no greater reward—no greater joy—nothing better.

I planted seeds.

I got a text later—she's talking with Jesus.

But here's why I felt compelled to tell you this story. Collaborating with God for the purpose of supernatural creativity will not be a walk in the park. Nothing *la-di-da* about it. Your creative walk with Jesus is going to require something of you. You will have the choice to respond; to submit; to go where you're not sure your feet can take you. It will require faith when things don't go the way you want them to; trust when you're convinced you're going to fail; perseverance when the going gets rough. It will take commitment on your part—an investment of your time, energy, and your hard-earned dollars.

But let me assure you. Even though it requires something of you, the benefits far outweigh the cost. There is no greater reward—no greater joy—nothing better.

It's yours for the taking.

Blessings and Love,
Jill Elizabeth Wyckoff

Author's Bio

JILL WYCKOFF IS an Encounter Artist who uses visual arts, performance arts, and the written word to encounter people with hope and healing. She is co-founder and Vice President of Kingdom Creativity International, a nonprofit organization that encourages, equips, and empowers people to discover and express their unique creative identity for the purpose of bringing hope, beauty, and restoration. She is also the Assistant Director of Kingdom Writers Association, working with writers of all levels to create redemptive works across all genres.

Jill works with both Christian and secular organizations to awaken individuals to their greater potential. She is passionate about encouraging others into their breakthroughs. She does this through creativity coaching, creative awakening retreats, customized workshops, theatrical presentations of her book, *Once Upon a Backpack*, and other creative ministry expressions.

An ordained pastor and follower of Jesus Christ, Jill is passionate about preaching the goodness of God and seeing people encounter the presence and power of the Lord. She and her husband, Brae Wyckoff, pastor a nontraditional church called The Exchange—a thriving community of creatives, curious ones, and truth seekers exploring Biblical truths through deep and meaningful conversations for the purpose of discovering and walking out one's true identity and original design.

Jill has three married children and seven grandchildren, all of whom are her absolute bliss. She and her husband, Brae Wyckoff, live happily ever after in Southern California.

If you would like to book Jill and/or Brae for a speaking engagement, visit www.kingdomcreativityinternational.com.

If this book has blessed you, please consider leaving an Amazon review and contacting the author through the above-referenced website. She'd love to hear from you.

Made in the USA
Middletown, DE
05 April 2021